WAR OF THE WORLDS

WAR OF THE WORLDS

SCREENPLAY BY
JOSH FRIEDMAN AND DAVID KOEPP

INTRODUCTION BY AND Q&A WITH
DAVID KOEPP

A Newmarket Shooting Script® Series Book
NEWMARKET PRESS • NEW YORK

The Newmarket Shooting Script® Series is a registered trademark of
Newmarket Publishing & Communications Company.

Manufactured in the United States of America.

This custom DVD edition is not intended for individual retail sale.

Retail trade edition ISBN: 1-55704-701-4

Library of Congress Catalog-in-Publication Data
Friedman, Josh.
War of the worlds : the shooting script / screenplay by Josh Friedman and David Koepp ;
introduction by David Koepp ; Q&A with David Koepp. —1st ed.
p. cm.
ISBN 1-55704-701-4 (cloth : alk. paper)
I. Koepp, David. II. War of the worlds (Motion picture : 2005) III. Title.
PN1997.2.W37 2005
791.43'72—dc22

2005024888

QUANTITY PURCHASES
Companies, professional groups, clubs, and other organizations may qualify for special terms when order-
ing quantities or special custom editions of our books. For information or a complete catalog, write to
Special Sales, Newmarket Press, 18 East 48th Street, New York, NY 10017;
call (212) 832-3575 or 1-800-669-3903; FAX (212) 832-3629; or e-mail info@newmarketpress.com.

Website: www.newmarketpress.com

OTHER BOOKS IN THE NEWMARKET SHOOTING SCRIPT® SERIES INCLUDE:

About a Boy: The Shooting Script
Adaptation: The Shooting Script
American Beauty: The Shooting Script
A Beautiful Mind: The Shooting Script
Big Fish: The Shooting Script
The Birdcage: The Shooting Script
Blackhawk Down: The Shooting Script
Cast Away: The Shooting Script
Cinderella Man: The Shooting Script
Dead Man Walking: The Shooting Script
Eternal Sunshine of the Spotless Mind:
    The Shooting Script

Gods and Monsters: The Shooting Script
I ♥ Huckabees: The Shooting Script
The Ice Storm: The Shooting Script
In Good Company: The Shooting Script
Magnolia: The Shooting Script
The Matrix: The Shooting Script
Pieces of April: The Shooting Script
Punch-Drunk Love: The Shooting Script
Red Dragon: The Shooting Script
The Shawshank Redemption: The Shooting Script
Sideways: The Shooting Script
Traffic: The Shooting Script

OTHER NEWMARKET PICTORIAL MOVIEBOOKS AND NEWMARKET INSIDER FILM BOOKS INCLUDE:

Amistad: A Celebration of the Film by Steven Spielberg
The Art of The Matrix*
The Art of X2*
Catch Me If You Can: The Illustrated Screenplay*
Chicago: The Movie and Lyrics*
E.T. The Extra Terrestrial From Concept to Classic—The
    Illustrated Story of the Film and the Filmmakers*
Frida: Bringing Frida Kahlo's Life and Art to Film*
Gladiator: The Making of the Ridley Scott Epic Film

Hotel Rwanda: Bringing the True Story of an African
    Hero to Film*
The Jaws Log
Kingdom of Heaven: The Ridley Scott Film and the
    History Behind the Story
Kinsey: Let's Talk About Sex*
Ray: A Tribute to the Movie, the Music, and the Man*
Saving Private Ryan: The Men, The Mission, The Movie
Schindler's List: Images of the Steven Spielberg Film

*Includes Screenplay

CONTENTS

INTRODUCTION

I GOT TO RIDE MY BIKE TO WORK
BY DAVID KOEPP

On this one, I was lucky. I got to work with Spielberg again and I got to ride my bike to work. In the end, those two things were the fun part of *War of the Worlds*, and as Fun Parts go, that's pretty damn good.

I've been writing movie scripts for almost twenty years now, and I spent the first fifteen or so of those years vainly chasing after the Fun Part. Only recently have I discovered that it was hiding in plain sight.

Movies, as somebody once said, are great big whales that need an almighty shove to get off the beach. At first, of course, nobody will help shove your whales off the beach, and you certainly can't do it by yourself. So back then I just assumed the Fun Part was writing the first draft, when it's just you and your ideas and your music and the clack of the keyboard when things are going well.

But then I actually got a movie made, and Ah ha!, I said, Get ready, here come the boatloads of fun. I figured the day I saw a film crew actually putting my scenes on film was the day the fabulousness would begin. And I guess it is, for some people, but not so much for the writer.

The problem is when you show up on the set, they're always doing it wrong. Sure, maybe they're doing it better—I've been lucky to work with some great directors; guys who can do it a thousand times better than I ever could. So it's better, okay. But it's not the way I saw it in my head.

Therefore it's wrong.

Eventually you learn it's probably easier if you don't hang around on the set, frowning and wincing, playing Word Cop. They're going to have to interpret what you wrote. Any director worth his salt doesn't just record what's written down—he's got to make it his somehow if it's going to be any good, and believe me, you don't want to stick around to watch that particular sausage being made. So shooting's not the fun part, not for the writer.

All the varying stages that followed also failed to reveal themselves as the fun part—not the editing, which is exciting, it's the last rewrite, but do you really want to watch someone else rewrite your stuff? Certainly not the shock of the preview screenings, and God knows not the release, when our brother and sister writers write reviews that claim the director and actors have miraculously made a silk purse of a film from our sow's ear of a script. And, of course, not the box office returns, which, *no matter what,* are always summed up with "Everyone was hoping for a little more."

I'm telling you, I've worked on the big ones and I've worked on the small ones, and everyone was hoping for a little more.

So after a few movies, a realization creeps up on you and you discover that the Fun Part might be what you thought it was in the first place, the beginning, the thinking it up, the first couple drafts when it's just you and your ideas and your music and the clack of the keyboard when things are going well.

I listen to a lot of soundtracks while I'm working—it's inspiring, and picking the right music for each project is a terrific way to postpone actually having to write anything. For *War of the Worlds* I thought a lot about Springsteen, those great stories of thwarted dreams and stagnant lives, songs like "Glory Days" and "The River." But I can't listen to lyrics while I'm writing—somehow the songs all end up in dialogue—so I shift to soundtracks when the first draft starts. On this one I played the shit out of Bernard Herrmann's hugely influential sci-fi score for *The Day the Earth Stood Still,* also Howard Shore's moody, foreboding music from *Panic Room,* and John Williams' *Saving Private Ryan* for a smidge of uplift. James Horner's *Pelican Brief* music vaulted me through most of the suspense scenes.

But inevitably, you have no choice but to type "Fade Out," and after that first draft leaves your hands, you're at the mercy of the world and a slew of moving parts over which you have little or no control. Despite my firm knowledge of how this all goes and my false modesty and warnings that "I know this needs a lot of work," the truth is I have never, ever, ever failed to finish a first draft that I did not secretly believe was going to be the first first draft ever greenlit and shot word for word.

'Cause you *gotta* believe that, at least for a while, otherwise how do you keep typing? Nobody's that mature. Not me, anyway.

So you send that first draft, with a fond little smile, knowing that your secret private time together with your ideas has come to an end. Film, as they drum into you the moment your plane lands in L.A., is a collaborative medium, relentlessly collaborative, violently collaborative, they will drag you off into the bushes to collaborate upon you, and if you're not prepared for that, you should dust off that novel you've been planning.

On *War of the Worlds* my honeymoon period lasted longer than usual. I gave Spielberg the first draft at the end of June 2004, and we started the rewrite process. One of the many wonderful things about working with Steven is that you *only* have to work with Steven, there's no committee to please, just one guy. One guy with a lot of ideas and opinions and more power to implement them than anyone in film, ever, sure, but everything is so much easier and more coherent when all those ideas and opinions are coming from the same place.

As a happy bonus for me, Steven was in my neck of the woods during that period, and his place was only five or six miles from mine. So, for the first time in twenty years I got to ride my bike to meetings, where the director would give me good ideas for which I could later take credit.

When I look back on *War of the Worlds* now, the moments I remember most vividly are the times I was on my bike, chugging up the last hill to the meeting, the script in my backpack, the exercise churning my brain and helping me cough up one or two halfway decent ideas, thinking, shit, this is great, I get to ride my bike to work.

If that's not fun, I don't know what is.

WAR OF THE WORLDS

screenplay by
Josh Friedman and David Koepp

based on the novel by
H.G. Wells

October 19, 2004

rev.		
	10-25-04	(blue)
	11-02-04	(pink)
	11-15-04	(yellow)
	11-23-04	(green)
	11-30-04	(goldenrod)
	12-03-04	(buff)
	12-09-04	(salmon)
	12-14-04	(cherry)
	01-06-05	(café au lait)
	01-20-05	(2nd blue)
	01-31-05	(2nd pink)
	02-16-05	(2nd yellow)
	02-28-05	(2nd green)
	03-31-05	(final)

1   SQUIRMING BACTERIA   1

teem before us. They're densely packed, thousands, maybe
millions of them, wriggling with abundant life. Pulling back, we
realize they're all contained in a single drop of water, and
pulling back further, the drop is one of many on a leaf, and we
think how truly insignificant those teeming bacteria really are,
because --

2   EXT   TROPICAL RAINFOREST   DAY   2

-- the leaf is one of a thousand on a treetop, and the tree one of
a million in a lush rainforest. Jungle animals HOOT, branches
bend as they're scampered over, the HUM of insects fills the air,
life is everywhere.

Heavy clouds part and all those billions of leaves turn upward,
stretching for the light that comes from the sun, a brilliant
orange ball of warmth, huge in the sky. The sun dissolves to --

3   EXT   BARREN PLANET SURFACE   DAY   3

-- *another* sun, and the contrast could not be greater. Where our
sun is full, rich, and hot, this second sun is tiny, small in its
sky, its rays thin and weak.

We tilt down to the surface of the planet below it. A frozen,
inhospitable plain stretches to the horizon, obscured by driving
sandstorms that must render life above the surface impossible.
There's some evidence that this wasn't always the case, thousand
year-old structures dot the surface, but they're abandoned now,
worn away by the relentless battering of the storms.

As for growth, there's only one type of vegetation tough enough
to survive in this hostile environment -- a scrabbly red weed.
It's mean and grasping, its sharp tendrils clawed into any
crevice it can find in the sand-blasted rock and buildings.

4   EXT   A MOUNTAINSIDE   DAY   4

Back on earth, springtime blooms on a mountainside. The sun
melts the winter snowfall on the banks of a stream, chunks of
melting white snow are swept away by the swiftly moving water.

High up in the air, we see the stream is part of a network that
feeds into a larger river, its banks swollen with the rich spring
runoff. This rich network of tributaries dissolves to --

5   EXT   BARREN PLANET SURFACE   DAY   5

-- a wider view of the surface of the barren planet, and a nearly
matching mountainside. But this one is dead, dried out rivers
carved into its face like acne scars. A VOICE comes over:

5   CONTINUED: 5

                         VOICE (O.S.)
                    No one would have believed in the early
                    years of the twenty-first century that
                    our world was being watched keenly and
                    closely by intelligences greater than
                    man's and yet as mortal as his own.
                    That as men busied themselves about
                    their various concerns...

6   EXT   SIXTH AVENUE   DAY   6

     One of those long-lens shots looking down Sixth Avenue in
     Manhattan as the workday lets out. People, scads of them, all in
     a terrible hurry.

                         VOICE (O.S.)
                    ...they were watched and studied, the
                    way a man with a microscope might
                    scrutinize the creatures that swarm and
                    multiply in a drop of water. With
                    infinite complacency we went to and fro
                    about the globe, confident of our empire
                    over this world.

     As we watch, the shot speeds up, turns into time lapse -- the
     people move faster, turn into the rush hour crowd, then thin out
     as twilight falls. We tilt up from the city as the last of the
     evening clouds race away, the moon rises and sets, the sky turns
     to night and dissolves into --

7   EXT   RED HOOK DOCKS   NIGHT   7

     -- a dazzling starfield, somewhere in outer space.

                         VOICE (O.S.)
                    Yet, across the gulf of space,
                    intellects vast and cool and
                    unsympathetic regarded this earth with
                    envious eyes. And slowly and surely...

     We pan toward one star in particular, a brilliant, hot white
     light.

                         VOICE (O.S.) (CONT'D)
                    ... they drew their plans against us.

     Drawing close, we realize it's man-made, an arclight on top of
     the spindly mechanical arm of a container handler on the docks in
     Red Hook, just across the East River from Manhattan. Down here
     on earth, huge cargo ships are unloaded by LONGSHOREMEN working
     the night shift.

7 CONTINUED: 7

We follow one container up, out of the hold of the ship, and look
up the cables of the crane that's lifting it, up to the windowed
cab suspended a hundred feet up in the air. There's a guy in
there.

8   INT   CRANE CAB   NIGHT   8

RAY FERRIER, the crane operator, is in good shape but pushing
forty from the wrong side these days, halfway through life and
feels like it's taking forever.

He's bent forward, looking through the clear floor of the cab,
studying the cargo container he's hauling as he skims the huge
crane across the dock far below.

9   EXT   DOCK   NIGHT   9

Down on the dock, the crane nestles the twenty foot cargo
container into the back of a flatbed truck, resting it gently in
a tiny spot.

The container BANGS down into place, the metal spreader that held
it de-couples and rises swiftly into the air.

A SIREN blows in the distance, loud. Shift's over.

10   INT   CAB   NIGHT   10

In the cab, Ray works the levers quickly, shutting down, hauling
the crane cab back to the top of the ladder that leads down to
ground level.

As it CLUNKS into place, he stretches out his back -- long shift
in that chair -- then reaches down into a bucket next to his cab
and grabs a chunky gold watch he puts there for safekeeping while
he's working. He SNAPS it onto his wrist.

11   EXT   DOCK   NIGHT   11

On the dock, the HATCH BOSS is waiting at the bottom of the ladder
as Ray climbs down from the cab.

                    HATCH BOSS
          Ferrier, I need you back in four instead
          of twelve, I've got half of Korea coming
          in at noon.

Ray jumps the last six steps and his boots hit the pavement. He
heads for the parking lot.

                    RAY
          Can't do it, I'm on a twelve hour blow.
          Call Tedesco.

11   CONTINUED:

                          HATCH BOSS
                Tedesco can't move forty crates an hour,
                I need somebody who can do double picks,
                c'mon, I'm in a position here.

                          RAY
                Wish I could help you, Sal, it's these
                Goddamn union regulations, whaddya gonna
                do?

He keeps walking. The Hatch Boss calls after him.

                          HATCH BOSS
                You know what your problem is?

                          RAY
                    (calling back over his shoulder)
                I can think of a couple women who'd be
                happy to tell you.

                                                    CUT TO:

12   EXT   ANCHOR INN   DAWN   12

The sun comes up over the Anchor Inn, a tavern nestled under a
freeway overpass near the docks.

13   INT   ANCHOR INN   DAWN   13

A pinball gets smacked around the table, BINGING off the bumpers
in a hot game.

Ray stands in front of it, working the flippers. He manages to
throw a hip into the pinball machine without upending the beer
bottle that rests on top of the glass. Unfortunately, the second
hip he smacks into the machine is a little too hard and the "TILT"
light lights up.

                          RAY
                Oh, for...

The flippers go dead and the ball rolls through.

AT THE BAR,

Ray reclaims his stool, between two other REGULARS. The place
has a horseshoe-shaped bar with a half-dozen PATRONS at it, all
night workers just off their shift at the docks. Ray looks up at
the BARTENDER, a cute, slightly hardened woman in her late
thirties.

>   RAY (cont'd)
>   I want my quarter back. You got the tilt
>   set too sensitive again.

The Bartender does not dignify this with a response. Ray shakes
his empty beer glass at her and the Bartender takes it.

>   RAY (cont'd)
>   I want my quarter back.

>   BARTENDER
>   From my cold dead hand.

>   RAY
>   Nothing cold about your hands.

>   BARTENDER
>   Sit down and behave yourself.

She picks up the remote for the TV that hangs over the bar.
There's a news report on CNN, we can't hear what the ANCHOR is
saying, but the graphic is fleetingly legible --

>   *Deadly Lightning Storm in Ukraine*

-- before the Bartender hits a button and flicks it over to
SportsCenter, which is doing a report on the Yankees' latest free
agent signing. (FOR FULL TEXT OF BOTH REPORTS, SEE APPENDIX A.)

>   RAY
>   I don't know, I don't know about this
>   guy, he hits what, .211 against left
>   handed pitching? And he has *never*
>   figured out Pedro.

A DOCKWORKER next to him shakes his head and gestures to Ray.

>   DOCKWORKER
>   Two years of double A ball and he thinks
>   he's an expert.

>   RAY
>   What we need is another arm. Shoulda
>   thrown money at that kid Santana in
>   Minnesota instead.

>   DOCKWORKER
>   Whatever you say, Yogi.

The Bartender comes back with Ray's beer, which reminds Ray:

>   RAY
>   Forgetting something? My quarter?

> BARTENDER
> Oh, for *God's sake*...

> DOCKWORKER
> He's never gonna drop it.

The Bartender opens the cash register and SLAPS two quarters on the bar.

> BARTENDER
> Like having my nine year old at work.

> RAY
> *Shit.*

Remembering something, he bolts out of there.

                                                        CUT TO:

14   EXT   RAY'S STREET - IRONBOUND   DAY   14

Early morning in a part of Newark's east ward called the Ironbound. Ray's block is mixed-use, a bodega on the corner, gas station across the street, other than that it's mostly working class row houses, close together, narrow driveways keeping everybody just about ten feet out of their neighbors' business. Although it's not that wide, the street is busy, lots of cars, it's that good shortcut everybody knows about.

Ray's fifteen year old Impala comes SCREECHING around the corner (keep meaning to fill those tires), and throws sparks as he pulls into a driveway in the middle of the block. As Ray gets out of his car, he waves to a brand-new Lexus SUV idling at the curb in front. Still got the dealer plates on it.

The front doors open. TIM and MARY ANN get out, dressed nicer than the neighborhood. Mary Ann is about six months pregnant.

> RAY
> Thought we said eight?

> MARY ANN
> It's twenty after.

> RAY
> That is one safe-looking new vehicle you
> got yourself there, Tim.

Tim just smiles, refusing to take the bait. He stakes out a position halfway between the car and the house.

> TIM
> Ray.

                            MARY ANN
              We'll be back by nine-thirty Sunday,
              depending on traffic.

                              RAY
              There he is!

Ray's looking past Tim, to the car. ROBBIE FERRIER, sixteen,
gets out of the back seat, backpack slung over one shoulder, G4
laptop shoved under one arm. Robbie's big for his age and not
used to it, his feet and vocal cords sometimes go their own way.

He walks toward the house as to a gallows, iPod earphones shoved
in his ears, BASSY RAP MUSIC so loud we can hear it plainly --
must be deafening to him.

                            RAY (cont'd)
                   (as he draws close)
              I get a hug?
                   (as he passes)
              Confusing handshake?
                   (as he goes into the house)
              Kick in the teeth?
                   (back to Mary Ann)
              Still working on those manners?

                            VOICE (O.S.)
              Hello, Dad.

Ray looks down. RACHEL, ten years old going on thirty, is
standing next to him, carrying a severely overstuffed American
Girl Travel Case.

                              RAY
              Hello, Rachel.

Rachel sets down her suitcase, opens her arms and gives her
father a half-hearted sideways hug (you know the kind), then
picks up her suitcase again.

                            MARY ANN
              Here, honey, let me give you a hand
              getting that inside.

                            RACHEL
              I can do it.

                            MARY ANN
              I don't mind.

                              RAY
              She said she can do it.

> MARY ANN
> It's heavy, I'll just get it in the
> door.

And with that she wrenches the suitcase from Rachel's hand and
heads into the house. Ray is irritated.

CUT TO:

15   INT   RAY'S HOUSE - LIVING ROOM   DAY   15

Ray stands in the middle of his living room as Mary Ann sets the
suitcase down near the base of the narrow flight of stairs and
takes a not-so-surreptitious look around the place.

It's not too clean. Or large. Or happy, for that matter.

Rachel sits on the edge of the sofa. Robbie is nowhere to be
seen. Tim lingers in the doorway, doesn't want to come all the
way in.

> RAY
> Better get going if you wanna beat
> traffic, don't you think?

In the kitchen, parts of a car engine cover the table. Mary Ann
notices, is less than thrilled. She opens his refrigerator.
Momentarily in profile, Ray can see her pregnancy clearly, for a
moment he just stares at her rounded form, so beautiful at this
stage. His face looks wistful for a moment, and then --

> MARY ANN
> You're out of milk. And everything
> else.

> RAY
> (hardening)
> Could you close the door, please?
> That's *my* refrigerator.

Rachel gets up, BANGS out the screen door to the tiny back yard.

> TIM
> I'm gonna wait in the car.

He leaves too. Mary Ann closes the refrigerator and picks up
Rachel's suitcase.

> MARY ANN
> I'll just get this upstairs.

> RAY
> Where are-

15   CONTINUED: 15

But she's gone, headed up. He sighs and follows her.

15A   INT   KIDS' BEDROOM   DAY   15A

The kids' room -- a pair of twin beds, two dressers, and not much
else. It shows almost no signs of life. The too-large TV set is
the only newish item in it. Robbie has yanked the mattress off an
old kids' bed that's carved and painted like a race car, he's
clearly outgrown it. He's sprawled out on the mattress on the
floor, iPod cranked, staring up at the ceiling.

Mary Ann stands in the middle of the room, sizing it up as Ray
appears in the doorway.

                         MARY ANN
              A little old to still be sharing, aren't
              they?

                         RAY
              I don't hear any complaints.

                         MARY ANN
              No, *I* do.

Robbie picks up the remote and CLICKS on the TV, to try and flush
his parents from the room. Mary Ann checks her watch, realizes
she's late. She gives Robbie a kiss on the forehead and heads
downstairs as she talks.

                         MARY ANN (cont'd)
              Robbie's got a paper on the French
              occupation of Algeria due Monday which
              he has yet to begin, it would be nice if
              he were done when we get back so I don't
              have to keep him up all night on Sunday.

15B   INT   LIVING ROOM   DAY   15B

Mary Ann comes down the stairs, followed by Ray.

                         MARY ANN
              We'll be at my parents' in Boston, but
              don't call the house line, you know-

She gestures awkwardly, apparently they don't like Ray.

                         MARY ANN (cont'd)
              Point is, I'll have my cell phone, so if
              anything comes up or you have questions,
              call me.

                         RAY
              Believe it or not I can handle it.

15B   CONTINUED:

She turns in the doorway and forces a smile.

                              MARY ANN
                    I'll leave the phone on.

                                                      CUT TO:

16   A TV NEWS REPORT   16

plays on a television screen, over another legend:

                Freak Lightning, Earthquake Strike Osaka

A REPORTER stands on a hilltop, a darkened cityscape barely
visible behind her on a very dark night.

                              REPORTER
                    -EMP, or electromagnetic pulse, which
                    causes a temporary interruption of all
                    electrical current within its field. As
                    in the Ukraine, there are scattered
                    reports that the EMP here was followed
                    by seismic activity on the scale of an
                    earthquake measuring 6.5 on the Richter
                    scale. This region, already hit hard by
                    a flu epidemic that has killed over-

POOF! The report goes dead, but only because someone has --

17   INT   KIDS' BEDROOM   DAY   17

-- shut off the TV that Robbie was watching, slumped on the bed in
his room.

                              ROBBIE
                    I was watching that!

Ray tosses a baseball glove at Robbie, who slaps it away.

                              ROBBIE (cont'd)
                    Baseball season's over.

                              RAY
                    Five minutes, it's not gonna kill you.

                                                      CUT TO:

18   EXT   RAY'S HOUSE - BACK YARD   DAY   18

A baseball SMACKS into Robbie's mitt. Ray threw it, and he's got
a good arm. Robbie throws it back, a half-assed lob that's meant
to irritate.

                              RAY
                    Call that a throw?

                            ROBBIE
                    Whatever, Ray.

Ray throws it back. SMACK! That one was harder.

Rachel looks up from the back steps, where she's playing with two
American Girl dolls.

                              RAY
                    Your mom says you got a report due
                    Monday. You're gonna go work on it when
                    we're done here.

                            ROBBIE
                    Yeah, I'm almost finished, I just gotta
                    type it up.

He throws it back, again too short, so Ray has to reach for it at
his ankles.

                              RAY
                    Bullshit.

                            ROBBIE
                    What do you know?

                              RAY
                    Everything. Haven't you heard? Between
                    me and my brother, we know everything.

Rachel chimes in, this is a familiar routine.

                            RACHEL
                    What's the capital of Australia?

                              RAY
                    That's one my brother knows.

Rachel laughs. Robbie does not.

                            ROBBIE
                    Okay with you if I just laugh the first
                    five hundred times you tell that one?

                              RAY
                    Just do the report. We don't send you to
                    school so you can flunk out.

                            ROBBIE
                    You don't pay for it, Tim does.

Ray throws it back, *really* hard, and it SMACKS into the palm of
Robbie's glove.

                         ROBBIE (cont'd)
              Ow!

                         RAY
              Come on, that's half what I got.

Robbie throws it back as hard as he can. Ray backhands it easily.

                         ROBBIE
              You're an asshole! I hate coming here!

                         RAY
              That why you act like such a dick?

Ray throws it back again, as hard as the last one. Robbie just
steps aside and lets it sail past him --

-- *CRASH*. Right through the kitchen window.

He gives Ray a look as cold as the North Pole, drops the baseball
glove on the lawn, and walks quietly into the house, letting the
door close behind him.

                         RAY (cont'd)
                   (to Rachel, who's staring)
              What?

                         RACHEL
              That's not how you're going to get to
              him. If you want him to listen you have
              to-

                         RAY
              What are you, your mother? Or mine?

He heads for the house, walking past her.

                         RACHEL
              Where are you going?

                         RAY
              To bed. I work for a living.

                         RACHEL
              What are we supposed to eat?

                         RAY
              There's money in my wallet. Order.

BANG. The door closes, leaving her alone on the back steps. She
turns her attention back to her dolls.

19   INT   RAY'S BEDROOM   DAY   19

Ray RIPS the blackout curtains shut in his bedroom, tears off his
pants and shirt, and flops onto his bed.

He fucked that all up miserably, and he knows it. He puts the
pillow over his head.

                                                    CUT TO:

20   INT   RAY'S - LIVING ROOM   DAY   20

Later in the day, around three. Rachel's on the couch in the
living room watching PowerPuff Girls with a glazed, four-hours-of-
TV look in her eyes. Takeout containers are spread out on the
coffee table in front of her, and half a dozen Briar Farm Horses
are lined up, taken from her open suitcase. One of them has a
yellow third-place ribbon around its neck. Rachel's huddled up
in a ball on the couch, hugging her knees to her chest, muttering
into an expensive-looking cell phone.

Ray comes down the stairs in a bathrobe and boxer shorts. He's
wiped out. GRUMBLES a greeting to her and heads for the kitchen.

                          RACHEL
                  (mutters into the phone)
              I gotta go.

She hangs it up and drops it on the coffee table with a CLATTER
without looking at Ray.

Ray goes into the kitchen, starts making coffee.

Rachel turns back to the TV, but her show is ending. She picks up
the remote and flicks channels, looking for another show.

ON TV,

she flicks past two more news reports about the lightning, but
she's going so fast nothing registers.

In the kitchen, Ray SLAPS the lid shut on the coffee maker and
pushes start.

Rachel settles on Nickelodeon, where a new show is starting.

Ray drops onto the couch next to her. She reaches out, turns one
of the toy horses slightly toward him. It's the one with the
yellow ribbon around its neck and she wants him to notice it, but
he doesn't.

>   RACHEL (cont'd)
>   I'm cold.
>
>   RAY
>   (shrugs)
>   Boiler's acting weird.

She shrugs back at him. He notices she's rubbing her palm, it
seems to hurt her.

>   RAY (cont'd)
>   What's the matter?
>
>   RACHEL
>   I got a splinter.

He reaches out, takes her hand and opens it. There's a sliver
buried deep in her palm.

>   RAY
>   Where'd you get it?
>
>   RACHEL
>   Your porch railing.
>
>   RAY
>   Want me to take it out for you?
>
>   RACHEL
>   (snatching her hand back)
>   Absolutely not.
>
>   RAY
>   It's gonna get infected.
>
>   RACHEL
>   No it won't. My body'll just push it
>   out. That's what I read.

She holds her hand tight, isn't going to let him anywhere near
it. Ray shrugs -- whatever. For a moment, they both watch The
Amanda Show.

>   RACHEL (cont'd)
>   You should get Tivo. Tim gave it to me
>   for my room, it's awesome, I can watch
>   my shows after homework.

Ray spots the half-eaten food on the table in front of them and
uses a crust of bread to scoop up some brownish dip.

>   RAY
>   I'll put it on my Platinum card.

He makes a horrible face at the food as the taste registers.

                    RAY (cont'd)
          What is *that?*

                    RACHEL
          Hummus.

                    RAY
          What the hell is hummus?

                    RACHEL
          From the health food place. I kept one
          of their menus last time we were here.

He stares at her as if she's insane while he tries to chew and
swallow that crap.

                    RACHEL (cont'd)
          You said order.

                    RAY
          I meant order *food.*

She reaches out and moves the horse a bit closer to Ray, brushing
the ribbon so it's facing him.

                    RAY (cont'd)
              (looking around)
          Where's Robbie?

                    RACHEL
          He went out.

                    RAY
          Where?

Rachel shrugs and mutters, pushes the horse away from him.

                    RAY (cont'd)
          What'd you say?

                    RACHEL
          Nothing.

                    RAY
          Where'd he go, Rachel?

                    RACHEL
          I don't know, he just took the car and
          left.

> RAY
> He took my *car?*

CUT TO:

21   EXT   RAY'S - STREET SIDE   DAY   21

Ray comes out the front door of his house, angrily pulling on a
shirt over a pair of blue jeans. Indeed, his driveway is empty.

> RAY
> You little shit. You little sixteen
> year old shit.

He walks to the street, looks up and down it. No sign of his car
or his son. But across the street, a GUY is staring at him.

And he's not the only one. THREE or FOUR MORE NEIGHBORS step
forward, drawn out of their houses to look at Ray, who puts his
hands out as if to say "what?"

But as they move closer, he notices they're not looking at him,
but behind him, slightly *over* him.

He turns around.

The skies behind his house are nearly black.

Heavy storm clouds are moving in, fast, faster than we've ever
seen storm clouds move. And they're dark, *really* dark, more like
night headed this way than thunderclouds.

A BRAZILIAN NEIGHBOR steps up next to Ray as they both watch the
skies.

> BRAZILIAN NEIGHBOR
> You ever see anything like that?

> RAY
> In the spring, maybe... not this time of
> year.

The Brazilian Neighbor turns and says something to his WIFE in
Portugese. She shakes her head and replies.

Drawn to the storm, Ray walks down his narrow driveway --

22   EXT   RAY'S HOUSE - BACK YARD   DAY   22

-- and into his backyard to get a better look, all the while
staring up at the sky. OTHER NEIGHBORS are going into their own
backyards too, and on this block the yards are close together,
you can see down ten or twelve of them all at once.

Laundry hangs off lines in many of the yards, FLAPPING in a
freshening breeze. A few yards away, a GUY WITH A POWER
LAWNMOWER walks back and forth, cutting his grass.

Ray turns and looks down the yards to the left. His NEXT-DOOR
NEIGHBOR, a woman in her late twenties holding a TODDLER in her
arms, is standing at the fence line. She wears a pair of metal-
framed eyeglasses. Her dress billows out around her legs, the
air is moving faster now.

CRACK!

A wet towel hanging off her laundry line SNAPS in the breeze,
which should now be called a wind. The laundry is standing out
nearly straight on the line, but --

                         RAY
              That's weird.

                    NEXT-DOOR NEIGHBOR
              What?

                         RAY
              Wind's blowing *toward* the storm.

-- it is indeed pointing toward the clouds, as if sucked in that
direction.

Ray looks the other way. *All* the laundry, in all the yards, seems
to reach out toward the storm.

Behind Ray, Rachel opens the back door of the house and steps
out. The back door, pulled by the advancing low pressure system,
SLAMS behind her with such force it cracks the frame.

Ray turns. Gives her a reassuring smile.

                         RAY (cont'd)
              Come look, it's cool!

Rachel walks forward, pulled slightly by the wind, like walking
downhill. He catches her, laughing. We haven't seen him this
animated before.

The clouds are nearly on top of them now, and the wind is blowing
so hard --

-- actually, no, the wind isn't blowing any more, in fact it
stops, suddenly, all at once. Nothing moves, not their hair, not
the Neighbor's lightweight dress, not the laundry on the lines,
nothing.

A few yards away, the sound of the lawnmower abruptly stops too, its engine dying. Ray turns. The Guy who was mowing bends over, looking at the thing.

In the alley behind the house, a car's engine gives out, the car rolls slowly to a silent stop.

The clouds are nearly on top of them.

> NEXT-DOOR NEIGHBOR (O.S.)
> Sure got quiet.

Suddenly, they hear a loud metallic CLANG from behind them. They turn and look.

A metal garbage can lid is stuck to the side of a car, defying gravity. They all look at it, puzzled, and as they watch *three more garbage can lids* lift off the tops of the cans they're on, fly across a driveway, and SMACK into the side of the car.

> RAY
> What the hell?

> RACHEL (O.S.)
> DUCK!

Ray does, and good thing, as a KID'S BIKE sails through the air and SLAMS into a chain link fence, sticking there.

The Toddler starts to CRY.

Rachel is standing right next to Ray, his arm dangling near her waist. She CRIES OUT as a blue bolt of electricity CRACKS out from his wristwatch and ZAPS her belt buckle.

> RACHEL (cont'd)
> Ow!

> RAY
> What happened?!

Ray whips his watch off and drops it, but instead of falling to the ground, it flies out and sticks to Rachel's belt buckle.

> RAY (cont'd)
> It's magnetized!

As he speaks, the lawnmower starts to move of its own accord, pulled across the lawn and SLAMMING into the side of a pickup truck.

Now the Toddler really starts to WAIL and the neighbor hurries inside with him just as --

> RACHEL
> What's that smell?

-- *a lightning bolt RIPS across the sky over their heads.*

It doesn't touch the ground, it just arcs between two spots in the clouds above them, but the CRACK is nearly deafening from the massive release of energy.

Neighbors GASP and SHOUT, pointing upwards, "Did you see that?!"

Rachel SHRIEKS and grabs on to her father, he hustles her over to the back door, where they stand beneath the overhang.

> RAY
> It's okay, it's okay!

> RACHEL
> I want to go inside!

> RAY
> A'right, go ahead.

But he stays where he is, wants to watch the show. Rachel takes a couple steps toward the house, then comes back. She doesn't want to be by herself.

Another lightning bolt CRACKS a jagged path in the sky above them, and the Neighbors who have stayed in their yards OOOH at the impressive display.

Still no rain, and oddly, no thunder either, just huge releases of energy over their heads.

A third RIP of lightning above them, and now the Neighbors CLAP, like at a fireworks show. Hey, this is fun.

> RACHEL
> (warming)
> Like the Fourth of July?

> RAY
> Yeah, that's it, like-

A MONSTER of a lightning bolt strikes, just behind the row of houses that borders their back yards. The smell of char fills the air, a dense cloud of electrified dust wafts towards them, and the SCREAM of whoever was in the vicinity of where it hit rips across the open yards.

22   CONTINUED: (4)   22

The fun is over. Neighbors run for their houses, some are still
laughing, but others are SHOUTING to each other to get the hell
inside, what's the matter with you?, and now it's as if that
first lightning bolt to touch the ground has released a flood of
energy, because suddenly there is lightning *everywhere*, arcing
across the sky, striking trees and television aerials and
flagpoles and clotheslines, even, it's a true lightning storm.

Ray throws open the back door of the house, grabs Rachel, and
hauls her inside.

23   INT   RAY'S HOUSE - LIVING ROOM   DAY   23

Ray SLAMS the back door and locks it (not sure why), runs to the
front door and closes that too, giving us only a momentary
glimpse of what's going on in the front of the house -- lightning
is leaping from car to car like an electrical virus.

But the door SLAMS and we don't see any more.

Ray runs to the kitchen again, where Rachel is curled up by the
back door, terrified. He bends down, grabs her by the shoulders.

                          RAY
                You're okay! You're fine!

                          RACHEL
                It hit right behind our house!

                          RAY
                Well, it's not going to hit there again,
                okay?! Lightning doesn't strike in the
                same-

CRASH! Another gigantic lightning strike, from right behind the
house. They twist over to the back window and peer up over the
ledge, where they can see out over their backyard.

24   THROUGH THE WINDOW,   24

the lightning bolt has, in fact, struck in the same place, just
behind that row of houses. As they watch, the bolt strikes
again, the same bolt, the same shape, the same place.

25   IN THE KITCHEN,   25

Rachel SCREAMS, Ray is stunned, and while they watch the bolt
strikes a *fourth* time, louder than any previous --

                          RACHEL
                Where's Robbie?!

-- a *fifth* time, louder still --

                              RAY
                    I don't know!

-- a *sixth, seventh, eighth* time, the noise is deafening,
maddening --

                              RACHEL
                    Is Robbie okay?!

                              RAY
                    (watching out the window)
                    Where's the thunder?!

-- *nine, ten, eleven,* it's never going to stop.

                              RACHEL
                    Why won't it stop?!

He grabs her and holds her tight as the lightning strikes
continue, over and over and over again, until finally it stops.

Ray and Rachel stay frozen under the window, silent, eyes like
saucers. Finally, as if to announce that it's really over --

-- all the magnets drop off the refrigerator and CLATTER to the
floor. That's weird.

                              RACHEL (cont'd)
                    Is it over?

Ray doesn't answer, because he doesn't know. It's darker in the
kitchen than it was before, the sun's down and no lights are on.
Slowly, Ray pulls away from his daughter and stands up.

                              RACHEL (cont'd)
                    Where are you going?!

                              RAY
                    Just to check things. Wait here.

She nods, backs herself up against the wall under the window.

                              RACHEL
                    Are we gonna be okay?

                              RAY
                    I don't know.

Ray stands, goes to the light switch and flicks it. But the
overhead light doesn't come on. He tries the switch next to it.
Nothing.

25   CONTINUED: (2)   25

                              RACHEL
                    You don't *know?*

                                RAY
                    No, I meant... please, just... stop
                    asking questions.

Ray looks at the clock that hangs over the kitchen table. The
hands point to 4:26. The sweep second isn't sweeping.

He checks his watch. It too has stopped.

26   OMITTED   26

27   INT   RAY'S HOUSE - LIVING ROOM   DAY   27

CLICK. Ray turns the switch on a lamp in the living room, which
doesn't work either.

He lifts the phone. No dial tone. He picks up Rachel's cell
phone from the coffee table, punches a button, but can't even get
it to turn on.

28   EXT   RAY'S HOUSE - FRONT   DAY   28

Ray steps out onto his front stoop and surveys the neighborhood.
It's quiet, unnaturally so, but PEOPLE are moving in the streets,
so at first it's hard to figure out the silence.

Then we get it -- the cars aren't moving. There's just as many in
the street as before, but they're all stilled, right where they
rolled to a stop.

A thin, acrid black smoke wafts over everything. Ray takes a
step off the stoop --

                            ROBBIE (O.S.)
                    Hey.

-- and nearly jumps out of his skin. Robbie is sitting in a beat-
up old lawn chair behind the door, leaning against the house.

                                RAY
                    Jesus!

He lunges at the kid, throwing his arms around him, an embrace
Robbie doesn't return.

                            RAY (cont'd)
                    You're okay?! Are you hurt?!

Robbie shakes his head no. His eyes are full of tears, but he's
trying like hell not to show it.

> RAY (cont'd)
> Where the hell did you go?!

> ROBBIE
> To get something to eat.

> RAY
> Did you see the lightning? Were you
> near it?

> ROBBIE
> (nods)
> The car just stopped. Then the
> lightning started to hit, about a block
> away, over and over. Me and another
> guy, we climbed under a dumpster.

> RAY
> Are you insane?

> ROBBIE
> What?

> RAY
> It's *metal*. Where was this?

> ROBBIE
> (offended)
> Over on Lincoln Avenue.

> RAY
> That far? It looked so much closer, I
> thought it was a block away.

> ROBBIE
> (shakes his head no)
> Over by the church. Twenty-six times,
> we counted. That's how many times it
> struck. It opened like this, hole,
> or... something. It was awesome.

Ray looks at him -- the brave face isn't very convincing, Robbie
must have been scared shitless.

> RAY
> Yeah, I bet.

Ray turns, looks around the block.

> RAY (cont'd)
> You hear how quiet it is?

>   ROBBIE
>   Power's out. Cars stopped. Everything
>   stopped. It's awesome.

>   RAY
>   Uh huh.
>   (starting down the steps)
>   Where'd you say it was? Lincoln Avenue
>   by the church?

He starts down the steps. Robbie gets up to follow him.

>   RAY (cont'd)
>   Your sister's in the kitchen, stay here
>   with her.

>   ROBBIE
>   *You* stay with her.

>   RAY
>   I can't, she's scared, she needs...

Trails off, can't find the words.

>   ROBBIE
>   What?

>   RAY
>   She needs *you*. Just stay with her.

>   ROBBIE
>   Whatever, Ray.

Ray starts up the sidewalk, then turns back.

>   RAY
>   And the next time you take my car, no
>   driver's license and no permission -- I
>   call the cops.

He joins the stream of people heading up the street on foot.

Robbie drops back into the chair and lets it tip back against the
side of the house with a THUD. His head is right next to the
doorway now and he turns to see Rachel standing just inside the
screen, looking at him, scared.

>   RACHEL
>   Where did he go?

                                        CUT TO:

29   EXT   RAY'S STREET - GAS STATION   DAY   29

Ray reaches the gas station at the end of his block. MANNY, the
garage owner, is in front, working under the hood of a late-model
car with another MECHANIC.

                         RAY
                Hey, Manny. What is it, dead?

Manny looks up, gestures around.

                        MANNY
                All of 'em. Everything. Look at that.

He picks up the starter, which he has disconnected and set on top
of the engine, shows it to Ray.

                        MANNY (cont'd)
                Starter's fried.

                         RAY
                Lightning hit it?

                        MANNY
                Not even close. Thought maybe if I
                changed it... you got any idea what's
                goin' on?

                         RAY
                On my way to find out.
                    (over his shoulder)
                Try'n change the solenoid. Mighta
                shorted...

Manny gestures, good idea.

                                              CUT TO:

30   EXT   THE INTERSECTION   DAY   30

Ray rounds a corner and joins a STREAM OF PEOPLE headed toward a
four-way intersection about a half mile from his house. Same
kind of neighborhood as his, but as he comes around the corner,
we see the difference --

-- there is a huge, jagged scar in the pavement, right across the
middle of the intersection. It's about twenty feet long, scorch
marks halo all around it.

There are maybe a HUNDRED PEOPLE there looking at it, most
huddled in small groups, comparing stories. (SEE APPENDIX AA FOR
DIALOGUE.) Nobody seems to have been hurt, and their initial
fear is starting to ease.

There are half a dozen COPS, but without cars or radios, they're
reduced to old-fashioned crowd control, which is not much. Also
A FEW PHOTOGRAPHERS, amateur and/or press, using non-digital
cameras, and a NEWS CREW cursing its useless video equipment.

Ray joins a couple guys at the edge of the group, JULIO and
VINCENT. They all know each other.

                    RAY
          I should have known you two were behind
          this.

                    VINCENT
          God is pissed off at this neighborhood,
          Raymond, I will tell you that much.

                    JULIO
          You see it?

                    RAY
          Yeah. You got power over where you are?

                    VINCENT
          Nope. No phone, nothin'.

                    RAY
          The *cars*, though, is the thing. You
          know?

                    JULIO
          Solar flare. That's what this dude over
          there told me he heard.

                    RAY
          Solar flare?

                    JULIO
          Yeah, he says the sun shoots off these
          big blobs of plasma, they turn into
          solar flares. It's the only thing that
          can kill all the electronic stuff like
          that.

                    VINCENT
          I got news for you, Julio, the sun
          doesn't make *lightning*, okay?

                    JULIO
          I'm saying what the guy said he heard!

Ray keeps walking, leaving this important scientific debate
behind.

He reaches the actual crack in the macadam and bends down to
investigate for himself. A few others are there too, running
their hands over the edges of it.

The crack is charred all along its edges, and rimmed with big
chunks of what looks like broken glass. Ray picks one up and
looks at it in the light -- it's similar to glass, but not quite.
He touches the edges, and they're soft, but when he bangs the
thing on the concrete, it doesn't break.

Weird. Ray reaches down to run his hand over the other chunks of
whatever-it-is, but as he touches the edge of the crack, a
strange look crosses his face. He lifts his hand off. Puts it on
again.

He looks at the GUY next to him, who is studying the damaged
street as well.

                          RAY
              Feel that?

The Guy puts his hands down flat against the edge of the crack. A
look crosses his face. Whatever it is, he feels it too.

Ray looks up. There's a parking meter a few feet away from him.
He studies it.

It's trembling.

Ever so slightly.

Ray looks back down. As he watches, a few small chunks of asphalt
break off the edge of the crack and fall inside.

Ray stands up, shoving the piece of "broken glass" into his
pocket.

                          RAY (cont'd)
              It's moving.

CRACK!

Ray whirls around. Behind him, the sound of CRACKING glass has
penetrated the still air.

He looks at the house on the corner, a narrow row house like his.
The front picture window has cracked, right down the middle. The
Crowd starts to SHOUT in alarm. (SEE APPENDIX B.)

CRACK!   CRACK CRACK!!

Ray whirls. Directly across the street, the picture windows of
several houses there are splitting as well.

The crowd, which had gone silent, is starting to MURMUR and
CHATTER when suddenly --

-- *everyone near the crack in the pavement is thrown to the
ground.*

Now there are some SCREAMS. It's especially vexing because only
those in a roughly circular area around the crack itself were
thrown off their feet. Everyone outside the circular area is
still standing.

Ray's on the ground, but he looks up between the legs of those
around him who are scrambling to get out of there, and he sees
that parking meter again.

Except now it's in the middle of the street.

The other parking meters are still where *they* were, in a neat
line on the sidewalk, but this one looks as if it has somehow
migrated out into traffic.

Pulling up above Ray, we see the sidewalk no longer follows a
straight line, neither the street, or the edges of the front
yards. A huge circular section of this neighborhood has suddenly
twisted three feet counter-clockwise, throwing everything out of
line.

There is great concern, but not quite panic.

Until the earthquake starts, that is. Because as Ray climbs to
his feet, that entire circle starts to rotate again, like a big
turntable, causing tremors that ripple out from its center,
spiderwebbing the pavement and sidewalks like ice in the
springtime.

The houses at the edges of the circle are ripping apart, right
down the middle, their facades tearing away, revealing cutaways
of the houses' interiors.

Ray, buffeted by the crowd as it flees the epicenter, comes eye
to eye with that rogue parking meter again. It's rattling
violently as it rotates around the edge of the circle, spitting
coins from the door in its front, which has sprung open.

A FOOLISH GUY moves along with it, scooping up the coins.

Ray bolts to the edge of the circle, which is now plainly marked
by the ruptures made by its rotation. Everybody clears it,
moving to the edges like soap flakes in a water glass.

The rotation stops.

People stop.

30   CONTINUED: (4)

Everything stops.

Silence for a second.

Those who still remain stare into the middle of the perfect
circle, which is now empty.

Ray looks at Vincent and Julio, who are standing next to him.
Nobody knows what to say. They look to the edge of the road, at
the now-cutaway facades of the houses, see a WOMAN in her
upstairs bedroom, staring in disbelief at her new view of the
street.

Okay, the buildup's over. Suddenly and with such force that we
feel completely unprepared, the center of the crack heaves up
into the air, spewing dirt, rock, and asphalt in all directions.

What's left of the crowd surges backwards, away from it, which is
good, because the geyser of earth that shoots out of the ground
is powerful and voluminous. Water mains SNAP like toothpicks,
sending geysers of water billowing into the air.

But still much of the crowd stays to gawk, standing in half-
fascinated terror.

Ray and those around him are knocked into the air and land hard on
their backs in the street. He sits up, but it's hard to see
anything clearly, there's dirt and water in the air and the
earthquake is still going on, everything is jarred, shaking, but
the one thing he gets a good look at --

-- *is the leg.*

Long, spindly, mechanical, it claws up out of the torn earth and
SMASHES down into the pavement just in front of him.

It's followed by a second leg, and a third, long seemingly-
metallic tubes three feet in diameter, telescoping in the
strangest manner we've ever seen, they seem to both expand and
collapse simultaneously, as if the metal were *flowing,* in and
out, over itself, in continual flux.

As each of the three legs plants itself at equidistant points
around the circumference of the circle, a bevelled pad irises out
of the bottom and claws into the earth, stabilizing itself.

Then, as one, the three legs WHIR to life and exert pressure
inward. From the center of the hole in the street, the earth-
smeared, squarish hulk of... *something* rises out of the ground.

It rests there on the surface for a moment, as if the long climb
out of the ground has exhausted it.

30   CONTINUED: (5)

Two portholes iris open on the side facing us, they look like
eyes on a face. Something rotates within them, as if the thing is
looking both ways.

Then the powerful legs kick in again and it begins to rise,
shoved aloft by its tripartite base, up into the air, ten feet,
twenty, fifty, a hundred.

Finally, it stops, resting at the top of its fully extended legs,
hovering there like a giant head on a pair of shoulders, peering
down at the utterly thunderstruck humans beneath it.

In this way, the first of the Tripods appears. It stands there, a
black silhouette against the sun, setting just behind it. It's
strange, though this thing is clearly hyper-advanced, in some
ways it looks ancient, full of stress marks and weathering like a
relic that's just been dug out of the sands.

Whatever semblance of calm there was before is utterly gone now,
whoever was left in the crowd backs off as far and as fast as they
can.

But there are those whose curiosity prevails, and Ray is one of
them. He falls back with a group of a half dozen, into --

31   THE MOUTH OF AN ALLEY,   31

-- maybe sixty or seventy yards away from the Tripod. They
strain for a look, shielding their eyes against the sun, which is
blinding behind the thing.

                         GUY 1
               WHAT IS IT?!

                         RAY
               JESUS!

                         GUY 2
               JESUS *CHRIST!*

                         GUY 1
               WHAT IS IT?!

                         RAY
               IT'S MOVING!

True enough, seen from their point of view, we see the entire
Tripod *shudder*, as if it just took a mouthful of hard liquor.
This movement shakes the last of the remaining dirt and rock from
it, they fall to the street and SMASH.

The thing just stands there again, unmoving. Suddenly, with a
sharp HISS, several vapor clouds shoot out of ports on the sides,
as if the thing is breathing.

And a fat spray of water bursts from its undercarriage, as if it's taking a leak on the street.

What the hell *is* it?

Ray looks around. Half the crowd is creeping forward again, not out in the open, of course, but in the mouths of alleys and driveways, behind cars, in doorways, half-sheltered groups of four and five staring open-mouthed at the apparition.

In the street, there is no one, no sound.

Except for a CLICK-CLICK-CLICK from across the street. A PHOTOGRAPHER steps from his hiding place between two houses and moves into the street.

From the side of the Tripod, a thin black whip emerges, maybe six feet long, snakelike. It stiffens and unfolds something flat and round from inside the head of the Tripod.

A SECOND PHOTOGRAPHER joins the first, they move out into an open area to get better shots of the Tripod.

The flat, round thing pivots upward, and it looks something like a small satellite dish, except it's perfectly polished, its surface brilliant and mirror-like.

                    RAY (cont'd)
          Get out of there! Are you crazy, get-

He starts to go after the Photographers, but a BIG GUY next to him grabs him by the collar and pulls him back.

In the street, the mirrored disk turns ever so slightly, trailing the Photographers as they make their way into the open, just watching them, apparently it means them no harm.

Ray breathes a small sigh of relief.

Now, emboldened by the first two Photographers, HALF A DOZEN AMATEURS move into the street bearing handheld videos, flash cameras, and the like.

The flashes FLASH, strobing the block.

Immediately, the mirrored disk pivots in their direction, what looks like a glint of sunlight flashes over it for the briefest of seconds --

-- and the Photographers simply evaporate, their bodies turned to dust, leaving their clothes floating in midair.

Ray blinks, he can't even register what's just happened, it was
so fast, one second ago two men were walking into the street, and
now they're, no, they don't even exist anymore, all flesh is
nothing but blowing dust now as their empty clothes waft to the
ground.

Now the full-fledged panic that has been building in the crowd
hits at last. *Everyone* takes off, bolting from their hiding
place, SCREAMING in terror.

Rather than tear ass into the open with the others, Ray remains
behind the corner of the building --

                         RAY (cont'd)
               WAIT, DON'T-

-- but those around him bolt, and his desperate grab can't hold
anyone back. The sudden movement of the crowd causes the Tripod
head to snap into action. It pivots quickly, seeming to brace
itself, and the mirrored disk rotates, sweeping once across the
street in a slow arc.

The air between the disk and the material objects on the ground
wavers, heat ripples like off the highway on a summer day, and
slowly everything before it is incinerated.

So swift and terrible is the heat ray's destruction that before
Ray can even back away, it's nearly upon him, wiping out the
building he's hiding behind.

Ray bolts into the street, just ahead of the heat ray. Behind
him, a FORTYISH GUY runs in terror in the same direction, toward
the safety of another building, just ahead.

Ray reaches the building first and lunges around the corner,
flattening himself against the building. He reaches out for the
Fortyish Guy and gets hold of his hand just as the heat ray
reaches that part of the street, it flashes, Ray tries to pull
the man to safety, he gets the Guy's arm around the corner --

-- just as the deadly heat hits him.

Ray pulls the arm, but that's all that's left of the Guy by the
time it comes around the corner. Ray SCREAMS and looks back in
horror, toward the Tripod. As he watches --

-- its legs suddenly *telescope*, vaulting the thing another fifty
feet up into the air, but that's not all, now up at this new
height, the horrible thing --

-- *takes a step forward.*

It can *move*. As it begins to stride forward, the heat ray flashes
again, SEARING into the side of the brick building Ray is hiding
behind.

As the brick begins to glow, Ray's attention is caught by a
FATHER in one of the split-apart houses, racing down the stairs,
holding one SMALL CHILD and dragging another KID by the hand.

Ray's eyes widen, remembering the kids, and he takes off, down
the narrow alley and over a chain-link fence at the other end,
disappearing into the smoke and haze.

32-35 OMITTED   32-35

36   INT   RAY'S HOUSE   DAY   36

BANG! Ray, covered in ash, SLAMS through the front door and
staggers into the kitchen. He gets there and turns in a half
circle, traumatized, not sure where to go or what to do. His legs
go out from under him and he collapses, cross-legged on the
kitchen floor.

Robbie and Rachel are visible through the open back door, staring
over the tree line at the mayhem in the distance. They hear him
and come into the house.

                         ROBBIE
                    What happened?

He doesn't answer.

                         RACHEL
                    Are you okay?

Still no answer.

                         RACHEL (cont'd)
                    Dad? What's the matter?

                         ROBBIE
                    What's that stuff all over you?

Ray gets up and turns to the sink, catches sight of himself in a
mirror hanging there. His face is covered in gray ash.

                         RACHEL
                    What's all that smoke outside? What's
                    going on out there?

Ray runs water and splashes it over his face, washing off the
ash. The cold seems to bring him back to life.

                    ROBBIE
          Hey! Hello?

  Ray turns back to them.

                    RAY
          We're getting out of there.

He goes across the room, finds Rachel's American Girl suitcase
and RIPS it open. He starts tossing aside school folders, dolls,
anything not absolutely necessary. He finds a sweater, shoves
that back inside. Also grabs another coat, hanging from a rack
on the wall, and shoves that in.

                    ROBBIE
          What? Why? What's going on?!

Ray grabs a loaf of bread and a couple apples off the counter and
shoves them into the suitcase, SNAPS it shut. He slides it
across the floor to Rachel, it hits her feet and stops.

                    RAY
          Take that and go wait by the front door.

                    RACHEL
          Where are we going?

Ray picks up a cardboard box next to the trash can, it's full of
paper for the recycling. He dumps the contents onto the floor
and shoves the empty box into Robbie's arms.

                    RAY
          Take anything edible in the refrigerator
          and put it in this box, plus the canned
          stuff from the cupboards.

                    ROBBIE
          What's-

                    RAY
          Do what I said!
              (Robbie hesitates)
          NOW!

Robbie sees the look in Ray's eyes, sees enough to know something
very, very bad has happened. He moves.

Ray opens a drawer and takes out a flashlight. He tries it, but
it's dead.

CONTINUED: (2)

Rachel, still puzzled, goes to the coffee table and picks up the
third-place ribbon, the one she was trying to get her father to
notice before. She puts it in her pocket.Ray rips open a fresh
pack of batteries and dumps them in the flashlight.

                              RAY (cont'd)
                    We're leaving this house in sixty
                    seconds.

Ray tries the flashlight again, now it works, and he tosses it in
the box. He turns and runs up the stairs.

Rachel, confused and alarmed, notices something out the open
front door. She walks over to it and stands in the doorway.

Outside, TWO MEN run past their house at top speed. Rachel
watches, thinks it weird. Their street, which was perfectly
peaceful thirty seconds ago, is showing the first signs of alarm,
but it's not yet widespread.

37   INT   RAY'S BEDROOM   DAY   37

Ray runs into his bedroom, drops to the floor next to the bed, and
pulls a metal box from underneath. It has a set of three tumblers
in the top. He spins them to enter a three-digit code and opens
the box, which is a gun safe.

Inside is a .38 and a box of bullets. He dumps the bullets in his
pocket, puts the gun in his waistband, and runs out.

38   INT   KIDS' BEDROOM   DAY   38

Ray grabs Robbie's backpack from off the bed.

39   OMITTED   39

40   EXT   RAY'S HOUSE   DAY   40

Ray, followed by the kids, BANGS through the front door of the
house. There is a good deal more commotion in the street than two
minutes ago, but on a scale of one to ten, the panic level is
still at a five. The first bits of news have come back about the
Tripod attack by word-of-mouth, but the full tide of news is just
about to hit.

Ray drags Rachel up the sidewalk, in the direction that HALF A
DOZEN SURVIVORS seem to be fleeing. Robbie follows at a half-
trot, carrying the cardboard box of food.

                              ROBBIE
                    What happened?!

                              RAY
                    Can't tell you now, we only got another
                    minute.

Ray looks ahead, to the gas station on the corner, where Manny
SLAMS the hood of the car he was repairing, which is now running.
Manny sees Ray coming and calls out to him.

                             MANNY
                    Hey, Ray! You were right! Had to change
                    the solenoid too!
                         (to the Mechanic)
                    Leave it on, run the alternator.

The Mechanic, who was behind the wheel, gets out, leaving the car
running. Ray quickly forms a plan, and he leads the kids quickly
toward the idling car.

Manny is at the corner, about ten feet away, talking with the
Mechanic, noticing the strange behavior of a few people in the
street, wondering what's going on.

Ray, Robbie and Rachel reach the car.

                              RAY
                         (quietly, to the kids)
                    Get in.

                             RACHEL
                    Whose car is-

                              RAY
                         (hisses)
                    Get in!

They do, Robbie in the front passenger seat, Rachel in the back.
Ray slides behind the wheel.

INT   CAR   DAY

Ray SLAMS the door. Manny and the Mechanic both turn at the
sound.

                              RAY
                    Lock your doors.

They do. Ray hits the window "up" buttons and the power windows
start to slide up, as Manny turns and looks at Ray, an odd smile
on his face.

He extends his hands -- "what's the joke?"

Suddenly and silently, right behind Manny --

CONTINUED:

-- *a maple tree bursts into flame.*

This is seen from inside the car, which perhaps makes it even more stunning and horrific.

The kids can only stare in stunned horror, but Ray drops the car in gear, hits the gas, and cranks the wheel.

The car spins a one-eighty in the parking lot, cutting around Manny, who has fallen back from the tree in horror. His Mechanic takes off running, but in the wrong direction, straight out into the street, toward the approaching chaos.

At the edge of the driveway, Ray SLAMS on the brakes, reaches in back, and throws open the rear passenger door.

He SCREAMS at Manny.

                    RAY (cont'd)
          GET IN!

Manny is standing in dumb terror, looking up at the tree, at the fleeing people, and at Ray.

                    RAY (cont'd)
          GET IN, MANNY, OR YOU ARE GOING TO DIE!

These are words Rachel has never, ever heard spoken in earnest. She starts to SCREAM.

Manny has a two-second window here to adjust to the new reality or cling to his old one and --

-- he clings, snapping out of his stupor with a look of fury.

                    MANNY
          Get the hell out of that car!

Wrong answer, and there's no more time for the right one. Ray hits the gas and the car SCREECHES out of the parking lot, leaving the furious Manny behind, SHOUTING at them --

-- *until he is incinerated by the heat ray.* His gas station busts into flame.

Again, the kids begin SCREAMING, but it's hard to hear over the racing engine, the SCREECHING tires.

Ray leans forward, trying like hell to see through the windshield, through the smoke that's now blanketing the block.

42   THROUGH THE WINDSHIELD,   42

      we see he's reaching the end of the block, which is a T
      intersection. Directly ahead of him is a bank of row houses. As
      we look at them --

      -- their second floors burst into flame, leaving the first floors
      intact. It's as if the heat ray were angled slightly, or coming
      over a rooftop and not able to point all the way down.

43   BACK IN THE CAR,   43

      Ray cuts the wheel hard to the left.

      Robbie turns and looks out the back window, gets just a *glimpse*
      of the top of the Tripod as it rises up over the rooftops behind
      them.

                          ROBBIE
                WHAT IS IT?!

                          RACHEL
                Is it the terrorists?!

44   EXT   EMPTY STREET   DUSK   44

      The car ROARS up an empty street, taking them away from the
      chaos.

45   EXT   FREEWAY ON-RAMP   DUSK   45

      Still the only car on the road, they SCREECH around a corner and
      hit a freeway on-ramp.

      We rise up, to get a look at the freeway. It's a massive parking
      lot.

      Ray steers their car onto the shoulder and they tear away into
      the distance. The sun has set, and dusk is starting to fade.

46   INT   CAR   DUSK   46

      On the freeway, there is a moment of quiet. It's otherworldly up
      here, though, the stalled cars WHOOSH by the windows fast; all
      traffic is standing still except for them. Lots of PEOPLE are
      still in their cars, many are standing on top of them, trying to
      get a look at what the hell is going on.

      But inside their car, they keep moving, Ray BLASTING the horn to
      try to get people off the shoulder ahead of them.

      Rachel is in back, eyes wide, sucking air hard through her nose,
      deep in a panic attack.

Robbie looks out at the swarms of PEOPLE as they ROAR past them on the freeway.

> ROBBIE
> Where are we going?!

> RAY
> I don't want to stop. We've got maybe the only working car anywhere around here, I'm not stopping until we're clear of it!

> ROBBIE
> Clear of *what?!*

> RAY
> I don't know.

On the other side of the freeway, a DOZEN POLICE CARS and FIRE TRUCKS race through the stilled traffic there, headed in the direction Ray and the kids just came from. (Apparently those vehicles are either still working or have been repaired.)

The SCREAMING SIRENS are deafening as they blast past. In the back seat, Rachel starts CRYING hysterically.

> ROBBIE
> What the hell is going on?!

> RAY
> You saw. We're under attack.

> ROBBIE
> By who?!

Ray doesn't answer -- how could you answer that?

> ROBBIE (cont'd)
> *Who is attacking us?!*

But Ray, trying to concentrate on driving, is unnerved by Rachel's hysteria.

> RAY
> Rachel! Stop it! STOP IT, Rachel!

But he's upsetting her more, and her CRIES turn to SCREAMS.

> ROBBIE
> (to Ray)
> You're freaking her out!

>   RAY
>   Do something!

Robbie climbs over the seat and slides in next to his sister,
comforting her.

>   ROBBIE
>   Okay, put 'em up.
>   (she keeps crying)
>   C'mon, Rachel, make the arms.

He holds his arms in front of him, making a space. She does the
same thing. Seems they've done this before.

>   ROBBIE (cont'd)
>   This space right here, this is yours.
>   This belongs to you. Right?

>   RACHEL
>   Right.

In front Ray tilts the rear view mirror, watching them. He can't
hear what they're saying, but it's definitely working. As Robbie
speaks softly to Rachel in what seems a practiced routine, she
starts to calm down.

In back:

>   ROBBIE
>   Listen... I'll be right back. I'm just
>   going in the front seat to talk to Dad,
>   I'll be, like, two feet away, okay?

>   RACHEL
>   (panicking again)
>   No!

>   ROBBIE
>   A'right, alright, just... just grab my
>   belt.

He leans forward, to talk to his father over the seat, and Rachel
grabs hold of his belt, to keep a hand on him.

In front, Robbie leans in closer to his father, lowers his voice
to a hushed whisper.

>   ROBBIE (cont'd)
>   I want to know everything you know.

Ray looks in the rear view, makes sure Rachel isn't watching
them. He too lowers his voice.

                    RAY
        This, this *thing*, like a machine.
        Climbed out of the ground. It just
        started burning everything. Killing
        everybody.

                    ROBBIE
        What is it?

                    RAY
        I don't know.

                    ROBBIE
            (a glance at Rachel)
        Is it terrorists?

                    RAY
        No. This came from someplace else.

                    ROBBIE
        What do you mean, like, Europe?

                    RAY
        Maybe it came down in the lightning
        storm. Maybe the thing was here
        already, buried, and then something else
        had to-

                    ROBBIE
        Wait a minute, what do you mean, came
        down? You just said it was buried!

                    RAY
        The *machine*, I'm talking about, is what
        was buried, what came *down* had to be
        what brought them up... brought up...

Ray just looks at him, can't bring himself to actually say "an
alien." Robbie returns the look for a long, puzzled moment, then
suddenly understanding breaks across is face and he grasps what
his father is trying to tell him without saying.

Robbie leans further forward and looks up, out the front
windshield. His eyes crawl up, to search the skies.

                    ROBBIE
        Why aren't there any helicopters? Or
        airplanes? Where is everybody?

Ray shrugs. He looks back at Rachel.

                    RAY
        She okay now?

                    ROBBIE
          Yeah.

                     RAY
          What was that thing you did with her,
          with your arms?

                    ROBBIE
          Works sometimes. She gets
          claustrophobic.

                     RAY
             (calling out to her)
          Rachel?

                    ROBBIE
          I said she's fine.

                     RAY
          You feel better?

                    RACHEL
          I want Mom.

                     RAY
          Yeah, I know, I just want to say... I
          need you to hold it together, you
          understand me? I gotta make a plan,
          figure out what we do --

                    RACHEL
          I want to be with Mom!

                     RAY
          -- and when you're screaming like that,
          I can't think, I can't-

                    RACHEL
          Mom! Take me to Mom's!

                     RAY
          Fine! Mom's! That's where we're going,
          okay?!, she and Tim probably turned back
          when they heard what happened, just
          gimme a break and-

                    RACHEL
          Mom! I want Mom!

                     RAY
          I KNOW!

She starts crying again. Robbie looks at Ray disapprovingly.

                         ROBBIE
                  Nice work.

He sits back again, to calm her down once more.

Ray looks up in the rear view, sees them both looking at him. The
look in their eyes is not one of confidence.

Ray looks out through the windshield. They've reached an open
patch of interstate. Night is falling, but aside from their
headlights, no man-made light comes on to pierce the gloom.

                                                    CUT TO:

47   OMITTED   47

48   EXT   UPSCALE SUBDIVISION   NIGHT   48

An upscale suburban block. The power's still on here and all
seems well, the streetlamps throw warm light on two neat rows of
McMansions. There isn't anybody out on the street, but that's
probably not unusual at this hour.

Ray turns into the third driveway on the right and Rachel
immediately bolts out of the car.

49   EXT   MARY ANN'S HOUSE   NIGHT   49

Rachel tears ass across the front lawn and up to the front door.

She pushes the doorbell, POUNDS on the door. Robbie's just
behind her, he gently pushes her out of the way and uses a key to
open it. The kids rush inside.

50   INT   MARY ANN'S HOUSE   NIGHT   50

The house is dark. Rachel flicks on the lights and runs inside.

                         RACHEL
                  Mom! Mom, where are you?!

                         ROBBIE
                  Mom?

No answer. Ray comes in and closes the door. While the kids
search the house, Ray sizes up the place. It's expensively
furnished, spacious, clean. Everything his place is not. He
runs a finger over a silver bowl on a side table. Notices a huge
flat screen TV on the far wall.

He checks out a framed photograph, a shot of Mary Ann and Tim on a
beach someplace, arms around the kids, *Ray's* kids, everybody
looking a little too happy.

50 CONTINUED: 50

Rachel and Robbie burst back into the living room.

                    ROBBIE (cont'd)
          They're gone.

                    RACHEL
          She's dead! They killed her!

                    RAY
          She's not dead, she's just not here.
          They were never here.

                    ROBBIE
          How do you know?

                    RAY
          Because they were on their way to
          Boston, they told us, this would have
          been completely out of the way, the
          opposite direction. They kept going,
          they're up in Boston at your grandma's
          by now.

                    ROBBIE
          I'm gonna call her!

He goes and picks up the phone, dials.

                    RACHEL
          How come the lights work here but not at
          our place?

                    RAY
          Because nothing bad's happened here.
          See, I told you, we're safe here.

Robbie, who's picked up the phone, shouts to them.

                    ROBBIE
          Busy signal -- one of those fast ones,
          the whole system's down!

He hangs up and immediately dials again.

                    RAY
          Everybody just relax, okay? We're here
          now, we're safe, we're staying. When we
          wake up in the morning, Tim and your mom
          are gonna be back, and everything's
          gonna be fine. Okay?

Unconvinced, they don't answer. So he answers himself.

50   CONTINUED: (2)   50

                              RAY (cont'd)
            Okay.

                                                         CUT TO:

51   INT   MARY ANN'S HOUSE - KITCHEN   NIGHT   51

A few minutes later. The kids are sitting at the table and Ray is
unpacking the box of food that Robbie hastily threw together.

Ray looks at the contents as he unpacks them, frustrated.

                              RAY
            Mustard? Mayonnaise? Salad dressing?
            What the hell were you thinking?

                            ROBBIE
            That's all there was in your fridge.

                              RAY
            Microwave popcorn, that's helpful.

                            ROBBIE
                (half under his breath)
            Dick.

Ray didn't hear that -- or maybe he did, and chose to ignore it.
He opens one of Mary Ann's cabinets and starts looking there.

                              RAY
            Where's all the food?

                            ROBBIE
            Mom gave the cook the week off.

                              RAY
            The cook, right, silly me.
                (shakes his head)
            She married up, your mom.

                            ROBBIE
            She sure did.
                (Ray looks at him sharply)
            What? You said it.

                            RACHEL
            What does that mean, married up?

                              RAY
            Nothin. Means she loves him.

He finds a jar of peanut butter and a loaf of bread on the
counter.

                              RAY (cont'd)
                 Peanut butter. Okay, good. We're gonna
                 eat sandwiches.

                              RACHEL
                 I'm allergic to peanut butter.

                              RAY
                 Since when?

                              RACHEL
                 Birth.

                              RAY
                 Just eat the bread.

                              RACHEL
                 I'm not hungry.

                              RAY
                    (to Robbie)
                 See if you can find a can of tuna.

                              ROBBIE
                 I'm not hungry either.

                              RAY
                 Fine.

            He throws the bread back, leans against the counter, facing away
            from them. Silence for a long moment.

                              RACHEL
                 Dad?

                              RAY
                 What?

                              RACHEL
                 What is happening?
                    (no answer)
                 Dad?
                    (still no answer)
                 Dad?

                                                       CUT TO:

            52 INT   MARY ANN'S HOUSE - BASEMENT   NIGHT   52

            The door opens at the head of a flight of wooden stairs and Ray
            starts down the steps into the basement. The kids follow him,
            carrying armloads of blankets and pillows.

                                RACHEL
                  If everything's fine, why do we have to
                  sleep in the basement? We have
                  perfectly good beds.

                                  RAY
                  Think of it like camping out.

                                ROBBIE
                  What are you afraid is gonna happen?

                                RAY
                    (looking around)
                  Who has a *basement* this nice?

It *is* nice. There's a Stairmaster, stretching machine, other
workout stuff, and a mirrored wall with free weights on racks.

Ray finds a likely corner and dumps the blankets and pillows.

                                RACHEL
                  I want to sleep in my bed. I have back
                  problems.

                                RAY
                    (getting exasperated)
                  Look, you know on the Weather Channel
                  how when there's a tornado, they tell
                  everybody to go down to the basement?
                  For safety? It's like that.

                                RACHEL
                  There's gonna be tornadoes?

Robbie rolls his eyes, annoyed by his father's mishandling of
her.

                                ROBBIE
                  No more talking. Lay down, Rachel.

He fluffs a couple pillows and Rachel lays down. He lays down
beside her.

Ray plugs a nightlight into a wall socket nearby, then comes and
pulls a blanket up over Rachel. She stares at him, eyes wide.

                                RAY
                  In the morning, we'll see what's going
                  on. We're safe here for tonight.

                              ROBBIE
                  How do you know?

                              RAY
                    I'm gonna be right in this chair over
                    here.

He turns and walks toward an old beat-up armchair under a window,
one of those narrow top-of-the-basement windows that is right at
grass level. On the way he bends down, surreptitiously pulling
something from Robbie's backpack, which leans against the wall.

It's the .38 he took from the gun safe under his bed. Hiding it
behind one leg, he turns and drops into the chair, sliding the
gun between the cushion and the arm of the chair, within easy
reach.

All of this he feels he has done on the sly, but when he settles
into the chair and looks up, Rachel is staring right at him.

                              RACHEL
                    Dad?

                              RAY
                    Yeah?

                              RACHEL
                    Am I ever going to see Mom again in my
                    life?

                              RAY
                    Yes. You are. I promise.

                              RACHEL
                    Tell me the other stuff.

                              RAY
                    What other stuff?

                              RACHEL
                    The stuff you don't want me to know.

He looks at her. The kid's too smart. He moves closer, sits down
on the floor next to her and tries his best.

                              RAY
                    Never could bullshit you.

                              RACHEL
                    You shouldn't use that language in front
                    of me.

                              RAY
                    Right, right.

He thinks. How the hell do you explain this one?

                    RAY (cont'd)
          Well, that... that lightning storm, it
          made the power go out, right? I don't
          know how, but it stopped all the phones,
          and TV, and most cars don't work. Now,
          another thing the lightning did is it...
          seems like it made this machine come up
          out of the earth. And that machine,
          it... it...

                    RACHEL
          It kills people.

                    RAY
          Yes, it does.

                    RACHEL
          How did the machine get down in the
          earth?

                    RAY
          I don't know.

                    RACHEL
          Is there more than one machine?

                    RAY
          No. Absolutely not. I only saw one, I'm
          sure of it.

                    RACHEL
          Well, who were the people who put it
          there?

                    RAY
          Let me tell you something I know for
          sure, okay? Wherever they're from, they
          have done a *very* stupid thing. I don't
          know what they expected to find when
          they got here, maybe no life, maybe
          nothing at all. But they found us. And
          they pissed us right off. And right now
          our army has found out about *them*, and
          they are very, very angry, and they're
          on their way this very minute to destroy
          that machine and whatever is running it.
          And then everything in your life, and
          mine, and Robbie's, is gonna go right
          back to exactly the way it was before.

She looks at him for a long moment, deciding whether or not to
believe that. Apparently satisfied, she rolls over, facing away
from him, and closes her eyes.

Ray goes back to the chair and slouches into it, breathes deeply.
He's about to close his eyes when Robbie rolls over, eyes open,
staring at him.

Ray looks at him. Robbie continues to stare. In the background,
we can see Rachel putting her arms out in front of her, making
space like she did in the car with Robbie.

                         RAY (cont'd)
                    (to Robbie, a whisper)
               What?

                         ROBBIE
               He died. That guy, Manny. He died.
                    (no answer from Ray)
               You stole his car, and now he's dead.

                         RAY
               You're alive, aren't you?

Robbie considers this, his face neither condemning nor excusing.
Just thinking about the new reality.

Ray breaks the eye contact, pulls his Yankees cap low over his
eyes and tries to get some sleep.

So ends the first night.

                                                  CUT TO:

53   INT   BASEMENT   NIGHT   53

Or so we thought. It's later. The kids are deeply asleep, Ray
lightly so. The nightlight glows in the socket on the other side
of the basement, a big round clock TICKS on the wall.

TICK. TICK. TICK.

The narrow window over Ray's head RATTLES lightly in its frame,
shaken by the wind.

Or is it the wind? Because the window starts RATTLING harder,
too hard for just wind.

Ray's eyes pop open. He looks up, at the pale moonlight coming
through the RATTLING window.

Ray twists in his chair, looks up at the window. He gets up and
stretches to look out through it.

THROUGH THE WINDOW,

he sees the trees in the front yard bending from a heavy wind.

IN THE BASEMENT,

Ray turns from the window, thinking. A hollow BOOM in the
distance draws his attention back to the window, and it's
followed quickly by a second BOOM, and then a third.

                    RAY
          Oh, no...

Outside the window, there is a silent, blinding flash of purple
light that illuminates the entire basement as if it were daytime
for a second.

Both kids sit bolt upright.

                    RACHEL
          What is it?! Is it the lightning?

                    RAY
          I don't know! I don't think so.

Another purple flash, brilliant and searing, it lights up the
entire basement for a split-second, and it's followed closely by
a tremendous BOOM.

                    ROBBIE
          What's that sound?!

                    RACHEL
          Is it them?! Is it them?!

They start to get up, but --

                    RAY
          Stay down!

Ray throws himself on them and they huddle into a corner.

The BOOMS grow louder, and the purple flashes, hot and irregular,
continue to flash into the basement through the window.

But this time another sound rises up over everything; this one's
like the SCREAM of an engine.

It starts out loud and gets louder, deafening, a HARSH METALLIC
SHRIEKING sound that is absolutely the loudest thing we've ever
heard in our lives, and it's building and building and building,
like a bomb about to fall right on top of us. On the far wall of
the basement, the rack of free weights starts trembling, tipping,
spilling weights that SLAM onto the floor around them.

53   CONTINUED: (2)   53

        Ray and the kids are SHOUTING and SCREAMING at each other, but we
        can't hear a word of it, and it sounds like that bomb is going to
        be right on top of us in a few seconds.

        Ray SCREAMS something we can't understand to Robbie, gesturing
        urgently. Robbie SHOUTS back, points to the other side of the
        basement.

        Ray leaps to his feet, dragging Rachel with him, gesturing for
        Robbie to go, quickly. Understanding, Robbie leads them all
        across the basement, further in, toward a metal door on the far
        side, he throws open the door --

54   INT   MACHINE ROOM   NIGHT   54

        -- and there's a staircase, down, and then another door at the
        bottom of it, a fire door, he opens that one too and they all fall
        into a deep, windowless room lit only by the flashing lightning
        coming through the open doors. We get just a glimpse of the
        inside of this sub-basement, it's full of pipes and tanks and the
        other junk that runs a house, then both the inner and outer doors
        SLAM, we're inside and in total darkness and --

55   IN TOTAL BLACK,   55

        -- *the bomb hits.*

        The explosion above and around them is so bone-rattling, and so
        close, that we practically lose our hearing for a minute.

        It settles, but we're still in darkness.

        Long moments go by. Outside, there are diminishing THUNKS and
        BOOMS as the residual explosions from whatever happened outside
        begin to fade.

        Faintly, we can hear fire. But that starts to fade too. Until we
        can only hear the breathing of three people.

        Breathing. Silence. Still black. Finally:

                            RACHEL
                     (a whisper)
                Are we still alive?

                                                          CUT TO:

56   INT   SUB-BASEMENT   DAY   56

        The next morning, not that we'd know -- the screen is still
        black. (We're going for a record for on-screen blackness here.)

56   CONTINUED: 56

          We hear the sound of someone waking up. A rapid intake of breath,
          a jerking sound, a GRUNT. It's Ray. At first, terror, he's lost
          in darkness, where the hell is he?

          Feet SCRAPE, he must be getting up. He fumbles around, searching
          the walls with his hands. His hands fall on a doorknob, he turns
          and pushes it open.

          Now narrow streams of light fall into the machine room. We see
          Robbie and Rachel are still asleep, slumped over in the corners.

          Ray finds something to prop open the door and looks up the short
          flight of stairs that leads to the basement. There's daylight
          coming around the edges of the door at the top of the stairs.

          Without waking the kids, he climbs the short flight of stairs and
          turns the knob. He pushes.

          But the door won't open. He leans up against it, puts his
          shoulder into it and forces it open about two feet, which is all
          it will give.

          Immediately, he winces from the brilliant daylight, but why is
          there brilliant daylight in the basement? His eyes adjust and he
          realizes --

57   EXT   RUINED BASEMENT   DAY   57

          -- the entire house has been wrenched right off its moorings.
          What once was the basement is now wreckage, the only thing left
          intact is the staircase that leads up to the ground floor, oddly
          spared in whatever catastrophe occurred here last night.

          Overhead, blue sky.

          Stunned, Ray picks his way through the wreckage and climbs the
          basement stairs, which lead up to ground level.

58   EXT   RUINED HOUSE   DAY   58

          Ray reaches the top of the stairs and stands in the ruins of the
          house. It's not so much that the house was torn down, more that
          it was sheared off its foundation, as if something reached down
          and swiped it away.

          We're looking at Ray, but something's obstructing our vision,
          something turning, spinning in front of us.

          All around, thick black smoke wafts through the air, and as a
          breeze picks up, it parts, revealing to Ray the source of the
          deafening explosion they heard last night, and finally we
          understand the apocalyptic sounds we heard were caused by --

-- the crash of a 747.

The entire tail section, nearly intact, is buried in the house
across the street, which has been decimated. We pull back, and
realize the thing spinning slowly in front of us is the turbine
of one of the engines, turned slowly by the morning breeze.

Wreckage is everywhere, the entire row of houses across the
street wiped out, either by the crash or the resulting fire, and
the debris field extends a hundred yards in all directions.

There don't appear to be any survivors, either from the plane or
in the nearby homes, an unearthly quiet has fallen over the
neighborhood.

It appears the plane came in low, right over this side of the
street, clipping this house and the one beside it, then crashed
on the other side.

But some things were oddly spared. The screen porch, still
intact. A bicycle, leaning against a tree. The stolen car still
in the driveway, thank God.

Like a sleepwalker, Ray stumbles forward, crosses what used to be
the street in the direction of the wreckage.

He stops short, next to an upright row of seats, five across from
the coach cabin. There are no corpses in them, but the seat belts
are all torn, the bodies ripped free.

Ray looks around. He calls out.

                         RAY
               Hello?!
                    (no answer)
               Anybody?!
                    (still nothing)
               CAN ANYBODY HEAR ME?!

He turns around and nearly jumps out of his skin as he sees a MAN
bent over right behind him, facing away. The guy's about forty,
his shirt's soaked in blood, and he's using a crowbar to try to
pry open a smashed and twisted food cart. He clutches a bandana
over his mouth to keep out the smoke and stench of the burning jet
fuel.

                         RAY (cont'd)
               Jesus, are you all right? Were you on
               the plane?!

The guy doesn't answer, just keeps prying at the cart.

                              RAY (cont'd)
                    I said are you all-

Ray walks forward and puts a hand on the guy's shoulder, and the
man whirls, fast, brandishing the crowbar.

                              VOICE (O.S.)
                    He's deaf.

Ray turns and sees a TV NEWS VAN that's pulled up onto the curb.

The back doors are open and a NEWS PRODUCER, a young woman around
thirty or so, is sitting there, shell-shocked. Her clothes are
torn and burned, and she's got a bandana over her mouth too,
which she moves only when she's speaking to Ray.

                              NEWS PRODUCER
                    A shell went off right beside him.
                    Camera on his shoulder saved his life.
                         (shouting)
                    You hear that, Max?! Your stupid camera
                    saved your stupid life!

Max goes back to prying open the food cart.

Ray chokes, gagging from the fumes. She tosses him her bandana
(which he takes and uses throughout the scene).

                              NEWS PRODUCER (cont'd)
                    Take this one. I'm used to it.

                              RAY
                    Thanks. Where were you?

She points behind them, to the west, where a line of smoke rises
on the horizon.

                              NEWS PRODUCER
                    Out there, in the Pine Barrens. We were
                    attached to a National Guard unit, the
                    83rd Mechanized. They moved on one of
                    those things around midnight. They've
                    got some kind of shield around 'em, you
                    can't see it, but everything we fire at
                    them detonates too early, before it gets
                    close enough to do any damage. Then
                    they flash that, that *thing*, and
                    everything lights up like Hiroshima.

                              RAY
                         (realizing with horror)
                    There's more than one?

58   CONTINUED: (3)   58

She gives him a look.

                        NEWS PRODUCER
               Are you kidding?

58A   INT   NEWS VAN   DAY   58A

BAM! The sliding side door of the news van SLAMS open and
daylight spills into its half-wrecked but still functioning
interior. There's shit scattered everywhere, they've been
driving this thing like maniacs, but the twin walls of electronic
equipment still appear intact.

The News Producer climbs in, Ray stands just outside. She talks
fast as she sorts through piles of three quarter inch videotapes,
pushing a few of them into machines.

                        NEWS PRODUCER
               There's a *lot* more than one.

She hits play on the first machine and a jerky, low-resolution
night-vision image comes up on the screen. Ray peers closely at
it. It's a battlefield, there's fire and explosions everywhere,
shot with a very long lens from far away, but in a brief moment of
near-clarity you can just barely make out the tall, spindly
shapes that dominate the field.

Tripods. Half a dozen of them.

                        NEWS PRODUCER (cont'd)
               We were feeding New York, but New York
               went dark, so we patched over to D.C.,
               and they went down.

Ray peers closer. There's an enormous amount of static and
interference in the shot, but there are flashes when we can just
make out what's going on -- the Tripods are marching through a
city somewhere, maybe downtown Newark. But whenever the image
becomes clear enough to give us a good look, the interference
wipes it out again.

                        NEWS PRODUCER (cont'd)
               L.A., Chicago, we uplinked to London,
               even called affiliates to try to get
               them to catch the feed, but nobody
               answers.

On the screen, a skyline is visible, it's definitely Newark, but
then there's an enormous amount of interference, and when the
image clears --

-- the skyline is gone, replaced by a smoldering valley.

       NEWS PRODUCER (cont'd)
    It's the same everywhere -- once the
    Tripods start to move, no more news
    comes out of that area.

Outside, there is an EXPLOSION in the distance. The Cameraman
SHOUTS at them from outside.

       CAMERAMAN (O.S.)
    We can't stay here!

The Producer hits play on the next machine and Ray moves in close
to the screen. Now it's shaky, hand-held footage from right down
in the thick of the battle, this must be how Max lost his hearing.

       RAY
    My God.

       NEWS PRODUCER
    You ain't seen nothin yet.

She hits "play" on a third recorder and another screen comes to
life. It looks like a mistake at first, it's just brilliant,
blinding flashes that blank out the screen.

       RAY
    That's one of the lightning storms, I
    was *in* one of those, I saw this.

       NEWS PRODUCER
    You didn't see it like this. Those
    things, the Tripods, they come up out of
    the ground, right, so that means they
    must have buried 'em here a long time
    ago. But who's *driving* the God damn
    things? Look.

She slows the image on screen down to a crawl, allowing us to look
closely at one lightning bolt in particular. There's something
in it, an object of some kind, a *thing*.

       RAY
    What... is that?

       NEWS PRODUCER
    That... is Them.

Another EXPLOSION in the distance, but slightly closer.

Remembering, Ray takes the shard of burnt-glass from his pocket,
the one he picked up earlier. He stares at it, thinking. It's
got some structure to it, like the bottom of a Coke bottle.

58A   CONTINUED: (2)

Like it was made, or forged, it's not a natural shape. He looks
from it to the screen, things come together in his head.

                         RAY
                They're in some kind of capsule. They
                come down in the lightning, they ride it
                down...

                         NEWS PRODUCER
                    (finishing his thought)
                Into the ground, into the machines. And
                once they activate them-

A third EXPLOSION cuts her off, as if to finish her thought, but
this one's enormous, and REALLY close. It rocks the van hard,
almost knocking them off their feet, reminding them they're still
in a war zone.

The Cameraman races past Ray --

                         CAMERAMAN
                We're getting the hell outta here!

-- rips open the driver's door and jumps inside. He starts it up
and guns the engine. The News Producer SHOUTS to Ray over the
ROARING engine.

                         NEWS PRODUCER
                Hey, wait a second, were you on this
                plane?!

                         RAY
                No.

The Cameraman drops the car in gear and hits the gas.

                         NEWS PRODUCER
                    (as the van rolls)
                Too bad! Woulda been a hell of a story!

She SLAMS the sliding door and the van tears away.

                                                       CUT TO:

59   EXT   MARY ANN'S HOUSE - WRECKAGE   DAY   59

Ray is looking straight at us.

                         RAY
                Look at me, understand? Don't look
                down, don't look around me, just keep
                your eyes on me.

Robbie sees it all and nearly chokes, trying not to vomit.

Rachel nods solemnly at Ray and he starts to walk her past the
smoking wreckage, sparing her the hideous sight. As they walk,
he talks soothingly to her.

> RAY (cont'd)
> We're going to Boston, sweetie. We're
> gonna find your mom.

60-64   OMITTED   60-64

65-65B OMITTED   65-65B

66   EXT   LOCAL ROAD   DAY   66

Their car ROARS down a deserted road, heading north. There are a
few other cars, but none of them are moving, they're pulled over
to the sides of the road, some left in the middle, but no people
to be seen, not a soul, not anywhere.

67   INT   CAR   DAY   67

Ray drives, Robbie's in the front seat, Rachel in back. Robbie's
searching for radio stations, but there's only STATIC.

> ROBBIE
> Why the hell aren't we on the highway?

> RAY
> I don't want anybody to see we've got a
> working car. We'll stay along the
> Hudson till we find an open bridge or
> ferry, then cross the river and stay on
> back roads across Connecticut.

> RACHEL
> Where *is* everybody?

> RAY
> Hiding in their basements, probably.
> Most escaped, I hope. But we're gonna
> catch up to them, I can tell you that.

Robbie leans over, lowers his voice so Rachel won't here.

> ROBBIE
> If we had any balls, we'd go back and
> find one of those things and-

> RAY
> (cutting him off)
> How about you let me decide when we
> fight?

67   CONTINUED: 67

                              ROBBIE
                    Which would be when, never? Never's
                    about your speed, isn't it, Ray?

                              RAY
                    Enough with the "Ray" shit. It's Dad
                    or, if you want, Mr. Ferrier, but that
                    seems weird to me. You decide.

Ray looks at him for a long moment. Robbie meets his eye for a
moment, then goes back to tuning the radio. Still only STATIC.

                                                       CUT TO:

68   EXT   THE MIDDLE OF NOWHERE   DAY   68

They've moved substantially further north, they're now in
farmland. It seems untouched by the battles that have raged
further south.

To the left is a seemingly endless corn field. To the right, an
untilled meadow. It's here the car slows and pulls over to the
side. The passenger side door starts to open, then abruptly --

69   INT   CAR   DAY   69

-- SLAMS shut. Ray has reached past Robbie, who was trying to get
out, and pulled his door shut hard.

                              RAY
                    Not so fast.

                              ROBBIE
                    I gotta *go*.

                              RAY
                    We got two things to watch for, and the
                    second is people who might want our car.

                              ROBBIE
                    There's *nobody* around!

Ray takes a long look around. The land is reasonably flat, you
can see pretty far in all directions. He relents, takes his hand
off Robbie's arm.

Robbie bolts out of the car, MUTTERING under his breath.

70   EXT   LONELY INTERSECTION   DAY   70

A few moments later, Ray opens the trunk and takes out a gas can.
Though the car is still running, he unscrews the gas cap and
upends the can, into the tank.

70   CONTINUED: 70

> Off to the right, there is a tree line about fifty yards away.
> Though Robbie has stopped short of it to go to the bathroom,
> Rachel is walking towards it.

                              RAY
                        (calling out)
                  Rachel! Right there is fine.

> She keeps walking, calls back over her shoulder.

                            RACHEL
              I'm not going in front of you guys!

> She keeps walking, toward the tree line.

> Ray watches for a moment, thinking. He looks around. They
> certainly are alone. He looks over the roof of the car at Rachel,
> who's nearing the tree line now.

                              RAY
                  Stay where I can see you!

> Rachel shouts something back, but he can't understand her. She
> steps into the trees.

71   EXT   WOODS   DAY   71

> Rachel enters the woods at the edge of the field. Looking around
> here, you wouldn't dream there's anything unusual going on in the
> world -- trees, sunlight, birds, rabbits skipping through the
> underbrush.

> Rachel looks all around, finds a likely spot, and is about to go
> to the bathroom when she hears a sound. She turns.

> Nothing threatening, just rushing water. A river. She walks a
> few steps more and looks through a stand of trees. Beyond, she
> can see the Hudson River moving past.

> The sunlight dapples off its moving surface. It's enticing. She
> moves through a stand of trees and comes out --

72   EXT   RIVER'S EDGE   DAY   72

> -- on its banks. It's beautiful. She looks upriver. It bends to
> the left just about fifty yards away. Rachel sees something
> float around the bend, something large and dark.

> Rachel's eyes widen and she freezes as the strong current pulls
> the something right past her.

> It's a dead body, floating face down in the river.

Rachel stares at it, transfixed, as it moves inexorably past her.
It's a man, or it was, in a business suit, but that's not what
catches her attention. It's his hand, which is still clamped
onto a leather briefcase, the fingers locked around the handle in
a death grip.

It passes, and Rachel lets out a breath of relief. At least it's
gone. She turns to look back upriver --

-- and sees *hundreds of bodies* float around the bend in the
river, bobbing swiftly toward her like a huge dead army.

She SCREAMS and turns to run, but there's a MAN behind her, he
grabs her roughly, she SCREAMS louder --

-- before realizing that it's her father.

                         RAY
              I said stay where I can see you!

                         RACHEL
               I'm sorry! I'm sorry, I'm sorry!

Ray looks up, just as the logjam of corpses moves past them. He
turns his daughter around, away from the carnage, and she buries
her face in his stomach.

                                                    CUT TO:

73   EXT   THE MIDDLE OF NOWHERE   DAY   73

The three of them come out of the field and are returning to the
car when Ray stops suddenly, holding up a hand. The kids stop,
look at him questioningly.

                         RAY
              What is that?

In the distance, a low RUMBLING sound is rising up. It gets loud
fast, REALLY loud. They all turn toward a rise in the road, and
the RUMBLING around them becomes almost deafening as --

-- *AN ARMY CONVOY ROARS OVER THE RISE IN THE ROAD.*

The three of them stare in wonder from the side of the road as an
entire mechanized battalion passes them by, a column that seems
to go on forever. Tanks, Bradley fighting vehicles, Humvee after
Humvee, dozens of armored personnel carriers, it's an awesome
display of military might.

Robbie runs alongside them and waves like a madman, SCREAMING the
unprintable things he wants to do to the invaders,
thankfully lost under the noise. Ray runs after him, grabbing
him and pulling him back.

> ROBBIE
> Let GO of me!

> RAY
> What are you, suicidal?

Robbie tears away and keeps up with the convoy. Ray pursues him
and both of them SHOUT over the noise of the passing trucks.

> ROBBIE
> I know where I'm going! I don't need
> you!

As a tank rolls past him, Robbie makes eye contact with one of the
SOLDIERS riding on top of it, his head and shoulders protruding
from the hatch. He's not much older than Robbie himself, maybe
nineteen years old.

Robbie stares, star struck, as the Young Soldier passes. He
grabs hold of a handle on the back of the tank, it almost pulls
him over. A SOLDIER shouts at him:

> SOLDIER
> Watch it, kid, you're gonna get hurt!

Ray grabs hold of Robbie and pulls him roughly away from the
convoy, stopping him by the side of the road.

> RAY
> You know what, the sixteen year old
> hardass routine is gettin' a little
> tired. I *know* what's back in that
> direction, believe me, anybody who stuck
> around to find out for themselves is
> dead! I'm not gonna let that happen to
> you!

In the background, we see Rachel start to pursue them.

> ROBBIE
> What do you care?! For real, you never
> gave a shit before, why start now?

> RAY
> Okay, you win, what's your plan? Come
> on, lay it out for me, you're in charge,
> what do we do?

> ROBBIE
> I'll tell you what we do, we catch up to
> those soldiers, hook up with whoever
> else isn't dead, and we get back at 'em!

> RAY
> Yeah, now let's try one that doesn't
> involve your ten year old sister joining
> the army. You got anything like that?

They're still moving, and in the background we can see Rachel
running now, racing toward them.

> ROBBIE
> Why don't you just tell us the truth?
> You have no *idea* which way to go. You
> wanna come off all wise and shit, but
> you only picked Boston because you think
> Mom is there, and if we find Mom you can
> dump us on her and you'll only have to
> worry about yourself, which is exactly
> the way you like it. Admit it, Ray, at
> least I'll respect you.

The convoy ROARS away, a cloud of dust receding on the horizon as
the convoy fades away to the south.

Rachel, who's nearly hysterical, catches up to Ray and Robbie and
SLAMS into Robbie, hitting him with balled-up fists.

> RACHEL
> Don't you leave me, don't you do that!
> Don't you *ever* do that to me!

> ROBBIE
> Rachel, stop, hey, *ow!*

> RACHEL
> You can't leave, you can't just run
> away! Who's going to take care of me if
> you go?! Who's going to take care of
> me?!

This, more than anything, makes Robbie feel terrible.

> ROBBIE
> I'm sorry. Rachel, I'm sorry.

He picks her up and carries her back toward the car, murmuring
softly to her to calm her down.

And you know, it doesn't make Ray feel any too good either. He
watches his kids walk away from him, feels horrible. Worthless.

Robbie looks back over his shoulder. He and Ray make eye
contact, then Robbie goes back to comforting Rachel, perhaps a
bit more tenderly than he even needs to.

Ray takes a deep breath and follows them.

                                                        CUT TO:

74-75   OMITTED   74-75

75A   INT   CAR   DAY   75A

The speedometer needle is on eighty and holding steady.

The car and its three occupants keep moving north, on another two-
lane highway. The skies are dark and a light rain is starting to
fall. Rachel, in back, has fallen asleep. In the front, Ray's
eyes are droopy.

Robbie is back to obsessively tuning the radio, but the digital
numbers just whiz around and around the dial, not even finding
anything to stop on.

Until, suddenly, it stops, way up on the dial, 108.6.

                    VOICE (ON RADIO)
            -- tuned to this station for updates.
            Repeating:

Ray and Robbie look at each other sharply. Robbie turns it up.

                    VOICE (ON RADIO) (CONT'D)
            You are tuned to the Emergency Broadcast
            System. This is a test. This is only a
            test. In the event of a real emergency,
            keep your radio dial tuned to this
            station and instructions and information
            will be provided. Repeating -- you are
            tuned to the emergency broadcast system.
            This is a test. This is only a test. In
            the event of a real emergency-

Disgusted and disappointed, Robbie CLICKS it off.

Ray, tired as hell, catches himself nodding off behind the wheel
and shakes his head, trying to wake himself up.

                    ROBBIE
            I could drive for a while.

                    RAY
            You don't have a license.

75A   CONTINUED: 75A

                                ROBBIE
                      When did that ever stop me?

        Ray looks at him, and a second later --

76   INT   CAR   DUSK   76

            -- he's behind the wheel, and Ray's in the passenger seat,
            asleep, head against the window. Some time has gone by, it's
            dusk now, and a heavy rain is falling.

            FOOM.

            Robbie turns abruptly, as a PERSON flashes past the car, walking
            by the side of the road. Surprised, Robbie turns and looks over
            his shoulder.

            FOOM. FOOM.

            Two more PEOPLE, walking down the side of the road.

            Robbie tightens his grip on the wheel. There's a growing stream
            of PEDESTRIANS on the side of the road, all carrying bundles and
            bags of possessions, all walking in the same direction.

                                ROBBIE
                      Ray.

            Ray doesn't wake up. Robbie's white-knuckle on the wheel. In
            back, Rachel looks out the window too. Seen through the glass,
            reflected off her face, there is a growing stream of displaced
            people. Many are on bicycles, some pushing stocked-up baby
            strollers or shopping carts filled with looted supplies --
            refugees, but this is America, these are Americans. Some SHOUT,
            wave, try to hitch a ride.

                                ROBBIE (cont'd)
                      Ray! DAD!

            He smacks his father in the shoulder, and Ray's eyes pop open. He
            looks around, wild-eyed, disoriented.

                                RAY
                      What is it?

                                ROBBIE
                      People. Everywhere.

            He slows to sixty. More people. Now to fifty. Not because
            Robbie wants to go slower, just to avoid hitting them.

CONTINUED: (2)

                         RAY
          He just wants a ride, that's all.

                         RACHEL
          Can we give him one?

                         RAY
          Sit *back*, Rachel. Put on your seat
          belt.

The crowd is really thickening now, the car slows to maybe twenty
miles an hour, and even that feels too fast, given the muddy
conditions. Ray clamps both hands on the wheel.

                         ROBBIE
          Be careful!

                         RAY
          I am.

A CRAZY GUY lunges in front of the car, waving his arms, but Ray
snaps the wheel to the right and fishtails around him, slipping
on the wet pavement, but managing to keep it on the road.

                         ROBBIE
          Where are they going?!

                         RAY
          The ferry, probably, it's just up ahead.
          But we're going all the way to the
          bridge, it'll be wide open and it's only
          another-

CRASH!

A boulder SMASHES into the windshield, spiderwebbing it. Rachel
SCREAMS, Ray and Robbie SHOUT in surprise, and Ray immediately
twitches the wheel to the right and punches the gas.

                         RAY (cont'd)
          Hang on.

He hauls the car onto the shoulder and takes it up to thirty or so
again, he can move faster here and the crowd is staying mostly
out of his way, except for the SHOUTS and JEERS and some pleading
CRIES.

                         ROBBIE
          DAD!

                         RAY
          I SEE IT!

                              RAY
                    Let me drive.
                        (Robbie brakes)
                    Don't stop. Keep the car moving, ho
                    your speed, just slide over.

He climbs over the back of the seat and comes aro
driver's seat. Rachel feels the movement on the
her and wakes up, blinking in confusion.

                            RACHEL
                    What are you doing?

                              RAY
                    Just goofin. Go back to sleep.

Robbie slides over in front, now driving with his
left foot on the gas. Ray slips over the back of
seat and back behind the wheel.

KA-THUNK. The door locks CHUNK down. Ray slips h
over his shoulder as he makes his way through the

                          RAY (cont'd)
                    Put yours on.

Rachel leans forward between the seats.

                            RACHEL
                    Where is everybody going?

                              RAY
                    They don't know.

                            RACHEL
                    But we do, right?

                              RAY
                    Yeah. We do.

The crowd's growing, marching toward a bottleneck
the working motor vehicle is arousing a lot of int

Ray slows even more, down to thirty-five.

THUNK!

Somebody has SMACKED the hood of the car with a bac
frustration as they drive past.

                            RACHEL
                    Why'd he do that?!

"It" is a tent that's set up on the side of the road, thirty feet ahead of them. Ray has to swerve hard, back onto the road, and the crowd is getting thicker and thicker now, it's all he can do to pick his way through it without hitting anybody.

They're getting angrier too, POUNDING on the car as it passes.

But suddenly, up ahead, there is daylight, a big gap in the crowd, and beyond that open road, as they all seem to be moving off to the right, down an incline that leads to the river.

Ray's eyes light up, he hits the gas, he's twenty feet from wide open road, ten feet, but just in front of him --

-- a guy pushes a WOMAN in front of the car.

Ray SHOUTS, cuts the wheel and slams on the brakes. The car spins, but Ray has just barely enough control to somehow, miraculously, cut a semi-circle around the Woman in the road.

The ass end of the car spins all the way around the front and SLAMS into a tree by the side of the road. Ray SMACKS his head off the driver's window, Robbie and Rachel are jostled but unhurt, and the car comes to a stop.

Ray turns, looks at them, disoriented.

                    RAY (cont'd)
          Are you okay?! Are you guys-

Suddenly, a GANG OF TEN descends on the car, BANGING on the windows with their fists.

                    RAY (cont'd)
          GET THE HELL AWAY FROM-

SMASH! Somebody's got a rock, and they hurl it through Ray's window. Glass flies and he recoils, his face flecked with blood from the flying shards.

Hands reach in, they're all in the car all of a sudden, Ray's door is unlocked, and he is dragged out.

                    ROBBIE
          GET YOUR HANDS OFF HIM!

                    RACHEL
          STOP IT STOP IT STOP IT!!!

Robbie throws his own door open and lunges into the thick of the crowd to try to protect his father.

The Gang of Ten (from all walks of life, the only thing they have in common is their desire to stay alive) drags Ray out of the car and throws him to the ground across the road.

The rain is really pouring down now, Ray is face down in the mud with somebody's knee in his back, no view of anything but feet kicking up the road around him, and the feeding frenzy that is currently taking place over his car.

Robbie tries to get near him but somebody takes a swing and it lands on the side of Robbie's face. He crumples into the mud.

                    RAY
          Rachel... Robbie... !

Somebody kicks him hard in the ribs and he coughs, spits blood. A stick CRACKS onto the back of his neck and his face rakes across the dirt.

A VOICE in the background SCREAMS at them to stop it, but we can't see who this decent person is, and can't hear much over the crowd.

In the midst of taking a beating from his faceless human enemies, Ray manages to work his right hand free from underneath him. He snakes it around, to behind his back, he reaches up under his shirt, his fingers close around something --

-- and all at once he rolls over, out from under the feet, pulling the .38 from the waistband of his pants.

                    VOICE (O.S.)
          GUN!

                    VOICE 2 (O.S.)
          HE'S GOT A GUN!

The Crowd that had gathered over him parts, revealing the sky for a moment, and Ray FIRES A SHOT, straight up over his head.

The CRACK rolls out over the crowd and they part, revealing his car again. Ray scampers to his feet.

Rachel is still in the back seat, MEN are swarming into the front, and Robbie, who has fought to his feet, is near the hood, fighting and kicking for all he's worth.

                    RAY
          Get away from the car.

There is a response, but it isn't quick enough to suit Ray's taste, so he FIRES ANOTHER SHOT into the air.

                         RAY (cont'd)
              GET AWAY FROM THE CAR!

Now the movement from the car is more panicked, the Crowd moves back, some putting their arms up in surrender, others urging Ray to calm down.

But he's in control now, he's got the situation in hand and all he has to do is-

CLICK-CLACK.

A loaded gun moves into frame, pointed at Ray's temple.

A GUY IN A SUIT holds the weapon, it's cocked and loaded.

                         GUY IN SUIT
              Put it down. I'm taking the car.

                         RAY
              My daughter's in there!

                         GUY IN SUIT
              Put it down!

                         RAY
              ALL I WANT IS MY DAUGHTER!

                         GUY IN SUIT
              PUT THE GOD DAMN GUN DOWN OR I PULL THE
              TRIGGER!

The Crowd swirls and SHOUTS around him. (SEE APPENDIX C.)

Ray drops the gun in the mud, it's pounced on by several more of the Gang, and in the ensuing confusion Ray is able to leap forward, to the car. (In the background, a guy in a BUS DRIVER'S uniform ends up with Ray's gun.)

At the car, Ray reaches around the front seat and unlocks the rear door, grabs hold of the petrified Rachel. Immediately, hands are on him and he is dragged away from the car again, but this time he's got a grip on Rachel.

Ray and Rachel are pulled back, away from the car, and fall to the road as the Guy in the Suit and two other LARGE MEN pile into the car. They start the engine, over the protests of some others in the crowd.

Arms locked tight around Rachel, Ray falls over backwards. He
turns and comes eye to eye with his own handgun, now held by the
Bus Driver, who has another eye on the car.

Ray rolls over, drags Rachel out of the mud and to her feet, and
moves away, toward the incline that leads down to the river
below, where most of the crowd is headed.

                         RAY
              ROBBIE?! ROBBIE!

                         ROBBIE
              I'M HERE!

Robbie follows them, they get just ten steps from the road, their
stolen car (now stolen again) starts rolling, but the Bus Driver
steps calmly up to the driver's window and --

-- POP! POP! POP!

The three men in the car are shot, the doors flung open, they're
dragged out and the car is once again swarmed over.

78   EXT   ON THE EMBANKMENT   DUSK   78

There are SCREAMS from the crowd of people swarming over the side
of the road and down the embankment, and now Ray, Robbie, and
Rachel are among them, without transportation and without
provisions, swept along on the tide of humanity, down the hill.

Ray is carrying Rachel, she's hugging him tightly, hysterical but
unhurt.

                         ROBBIE
              Where are we going?!

Up ahead, they hear SOOTHING MUSIC wafting strangely through the
trees. The people around them hear it too, they all press
forward, drawn.

                         RAY
              We're gonna be okay!

                         ROBBIE
              WHERE ARE WE GOING?!

                         RAY
              It's there! It's working! SEE?!

Robbie looks ahead, and our vision sweeps that way too. Down the
embankment, they're approaching the edge of the Hudson River, and
there, moored at the dock, its massive ENGINES HUMMING --

79   EXT   FERRY LANDING   NIGHT   79

-- is the Hudson Highland Ferry. The river's not terribly wide
at this point, but it's swift and dangerous. Just a mile or two
to the north, we can see the massive spans of the great bridge Ray
had hoped to make it to, but without a car the ferry is now their
only hope to get across.

Night has fallen, and the rain drizzles to a stop. The MUSIC they
heard is louder here, played through the boat's tinny speakers,
perhaps to soothe the panicky crowd. A FERRY WORKER is SHOUTING
to the crowd through cupped hands.

                    FERRY WORKER
              Please move forward calmly... there is
              room for everyone, and the boat can make
              more than one trip... Please, move
              forward calmly...

For the most part, the message is getting through. The crowd is
huge, but the boat is too, and there's no real sense of urgency.
The further they get downhill from the road, the more the
shooting at the car is left behind them.

As the crowd thickens, they notice people holding up hand-drawn
fliers, showing pictures of loved ones, searching for the
missing. Light poles are plastered with similar fliers, and
since the power's out, they're all made by hand, with real
photographs taped to them.

A DINGING sound gets their attention and the crowd stops, looking
around. A set of railroad crossing barriers descends right in
front of them and, looking down, they realize a set of railroad
tracks runs between them and the ferry landing.

The crowd looks around, waiting for the train to come, and it
arrives suddenly, all at once, barreling toward them at a hundred
miles an hour.

And it's on fire.

A shocked silence falls over the crowd as the burning passenger
train flies past them, a runaway, flames spewing from every
window, completely out of control. No sign of life is visible
within, and, as quickly as it appeared, it flies past them,
rocketing around a bend in a puff of smoke.

The gates rise, and the crowd pushes toward the ferry again.

79A   EXT   ON THE DOCK   NIGHT   79A

They reach the edge of the dock and step onto it. It's tighter
here, the Crowd has to bottleneck a little bit, but people are
still being cool about it. The MUSIC is louder.

                         RACHEL
                The power's still on here?

                         RAY
                Looks like it. Nothing came out of the
                ground here.

At the edge of the dock, there's a Red Cross blood drive booth set
up, it's staffed by HALF A DOZEN VOLUNTEERS, but they're turning
crowds away.

                         VOLUNTEER
                    (through a megaphone)
                Unless you are O positive and RH
                negative, thank you very much, but we
                already have more blood than we can use.
                Again, if you are O positive, RH
                negative, please identify yourself, if
                you are not, thank you very much but we
                already have more blood than people who
                need transfusions. Once again --

And it goes on, as they move past the booth. Nearby them, a GUY
WITH A TRANSISTOR RADIO has replaced the battery and got it
working again, unfortunately there's nothing but STATIC all over
the dial.

We start in close on the dial as it twists through the stations,
finding no information there. Pulling up from it, we follow Ray,
Rachel and Robbie as they move through the crowd, down the
hillside toward the dock. As they go they overhear murmurs,
whisperings, snatches of conversations, the only information
anybody can glean about what exactly is going on:

                         OLDER MAN
                We've got it the worst here, that's what
                I heard. The U.S. mostly, South America
                and Asia some. There's nothing
                happening in Europe.

                         YOUNGER MAN
                Really? That's not what I heard.

                         OLDER MAN
                You heard wrong, it's mostly here. Of
                course they came after us first.

Now a quick fragment from behind them:

                          FRAGMENT GUY 1
                   -we're supposed to meet in New London-

They keep moving, passing a WOMAN clutching a tattered yellow
flyer:

                          LADY FROM UPSTATE
                   We were outside Albany, the planes flew
                   in low and dropped these, there's a food
                   drop, it says, just over the Connecticut
                   border, tomorrow morning, and first aid
                   stations, they're opening them all up
                   and down the Hudson...

A PANICKY GUY passes in front of them, beseeching everyone:

                          PANICKY GUY
                   -the top of the hill about five minutes
                   ago, please, did you see him? He's
                   eighty years old, he's about six feet
                   tall, he's got white hair and a bright
                   blue jacket-

They keep moving, passing into another conversation. An
INFORMATIVE GUY is talking the ears off a WORRIED FATHER who's
with his WIFE and LITTLE KIDS.

                          INFORMATIVE GUY
                   No information, that's what's got me
                   crazy, nobody really knows anything,
                   just the stuff they're making up to make
                   themselves feel better!

The Worried Father, who's been nodding, listening, turns away to
his Wife, away from the Informative Guy.

                          WIFE
                   What'd he say?!

                          WORRIED FATHER
                   He doesn't know anything.

Another quick fragment:

                          FRAGMENT GUY 2
                   -they'll protect anybody who can make it
                   to the submarine base-

Ray, Rachel and Robbie keep moving, through the crowd, into still
more talk:

> ILL-INFORMED GUY
> Europe got it worst of all, that's what
> everybody's saying. Completely wiped
> out, some of it, full-scale invasion.

> CONSPIRACY BUFF
> Invasion? There's no invasion, it's *us,*
> the government.

> CONSPIRACY DEBUNKER
> You're kidding yourself, there's no
> government, there's no order, there's
> nobody in charge-

> CONSPIRACY BUFF
> They're trying to scare us, pump up our
> fear so we'll roll over for 'em.

> DOOMSDAY GUY
> I don't give a shit who it is, I got up
> close to one of those things in
> Stanfordville, if they're all over the
> place we're dead, we're all dead.

> UPSET MOTHER
> Can you *please* not have this
> conversation in front of the children!?

Ray notices Rachel, who's vastly concerned by all the
conversations going on around them. He draws her attention:

> RAY
> Rach? Rachel, look... we're getting on
> the boat... we're gonna make it.

Rachel lifts her head off his shoulder and turns around, sees
that they are, indeed, getting on the boat. This seems to help.

Ray kisses her on the forehead and wipes away her tears.

> RAY (cont'd)
> Nothing bad is gonna happen to you. I
> promise, Sweetie.

Rachel nods, calming. Next to them, a MOTHER carrying a THREE
YEAR OLD is feeding a cereal bar to him. She notices Rachel
looking at the bar. She whispers in the Three Year Old's ear, he
looks up at Rachel too.

The Mother takes the cereal bar, breaks it in half and holds it
out to Rachel.

STILLS

Captions by David Koepp

The crowd surges toward the ferry. This was some of the best direction of extras I have ever seen, bar none. The fact that no one was hurt in this stampede is incredible.

Tom Cruise (opposite) as Ray Ferrier, Dakota Fanning (above) as Rachel, and Justin Chatwin (below) as Robbie. I figured Ray was one of those athlete-egomaniac guys when he was young and wanted all his kids' names to start with his initial.

Miranda Otto (above) as Ray's ex-wife Mary Ann. Tim Robbins (below) as Harlan Ogilvy, an amalgam of two characters from Wells' novel, with a name cribbed from a third.

David Alan Basche (left) as Tim, Mary Ann's second husband. Looks thrilled to be at Ray's place, doesn't he?

Above: Ray and Rachel watching the storm come in. I liked Ray's juvenile excitement here, even when his daughter's freaking out. Below: Ray doesn't think it's so funny anymore. Opposite: The location that production designer Rick Carter found for the intersection scene is one of my favorite things in the movie, and the church made a nice reference to the 1953 film.

Above: Ray's covered in dust from the attack in the intersection. Opposite, above: The idea that Rachel looks to her brother for comfort instead of her father was painful, accurate, and not mine. Spielberg really knows his way around family drama. Opposite, below: One of our finest American actors, and she's only eleven. Don't tell her how good she is. Following page: Dennis Muren's tripods return to ruin everything. Only Edith Head has more Oscars than this guy, but hey, Dennis is still in his prime. She's toast.

Above and below: The movie was originally planned for summer weather, but the change to winter added snow, bare trees, and freezing cold. Nasty for the shoot; great for the look. Opposite: Steven wanted the tripods to have two giant lights located underneath the hood of the top portion. They looked like eyes, of course, and helped anthropomorphize our monster machines.

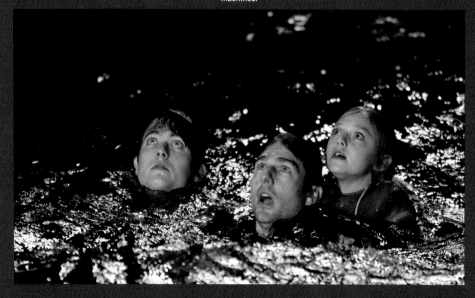

Above: More bare trees and mayhem. The decision to stay on this side of the ridge and never see the full battle was classic Spielberg. Below, left: That's Ogilvy's wedding ring he's wearing around his neck, a tribute to his dead wife. Below, right: The tunneling idea is based on the Artilleryman's grand, futile plans in the novel. Following page: Red weed everywhere. There's a great line from the novel: "He stepped out into the weird and lurid landscape of another world."

Above: The crowd and army descend on a fallen tripod. Below, left and right: Ray returns Rachel to her grateful grandparents, played by Gene Barry and Ann Robinson, who starred in the 1953 film.

Above: An artist's rendering of the destruction of the church. Below: The sinking of the ferry. It's amazing how closely the finished film resembles these early sketches.

Above and below: Same again here, the finished version is remarkably similar. The ability to get the images in your head onto film is what defines you as a director.

Above: Steven putting together the remarkable single shot that takes in the entire basement and plays two or three pages of dialogue in one well-choreographed move. Below: That's me with Steven.

Above: Janusz Kaminski, the director of photography. His matching of mood to content is flawless throughout the movie, if you ask me. Below: Steven confers with effects designer Dennis Muren. When I work on a movie that Dennis will be doing, I try to think of impossible images to make his life miserable. But you can't stump this band.

Two guys who need no introduction...

Rachel smiles and takes it. Ray looks at the Mother, grateful,
almost overwhelmed by the tiny gesture. He nods at her, she
smiles back.

Ray looks at Robbie, who is next to him. He gives him a wink.
Robbie grins tightly, exhales, calming. They've made it. This
far, anyway.

Rachel turns back, to rest her head on her father's shoulder,
chewing contentedly on the cereal bar. A flock of seagulls flies
low over them, and Rachel's eyes follow them as they head up the
embankment.

She sees something behind them and her eyes narrow.

She lifts her head. She cocks it sideways -- huh?

Ray turns, and does a double take looking at the crowd, as he sees
a familiar face -- it's the Bartender from the bar at the
beginning, the woman in her late thirties. She's across the
crowd from him, maybe twenty yards, clutching the hand of a NINE
YEAR OLD BOY.

Ray waves a hand in surprised greeting, she recognizes him and
smiles. Ray starts to say something, but is interrupted by
Rachel --

                         RACHEL
              The trees are funny.

She's looking back up the hill.

Ray turns away from the Bartender, to follow Rachel's gaze. Up
at the top of the embankment, there is a row of tall trees, the
forest runs all the way to the Highlands Road, which is what they
drove in on.

The seagulls are darting into the trees, up on the highlands,
which do indeed look funny. They seem to be *breathing*, a strange
mist emanating from inside them.And they're *moving*. But moving
forward, in a most un-treelike manner. Three of them, anyway.

Ray's face goes white, fifty heads around him turn --

-- *AND A TRIPOD STEPS OUT OF THE FOREST.*

For a moment, absolutely everything stops, no sound, no movement,
no nothing, and the Tripod just stands there, its head-like top
staring down at the crowd as it swarms toward the ferry boat,
emanating clouds of vapor as it did in the street back in Ray's
neighborhood.

Robbie and Rachel, who never saw the Tripod back on Ray's block, stare at it, horror-struck.

The seagulls swarm around the head of the Tripod like moths around a flame.

On the dock, panic hits. Ray turns back to where the Bartender was, but all he sees is the whites of her wide-open eyes as she and her son are swept away by the panicking crowd, which surges forward, pushing to get onto the boat. The Captain hits the engines, they ROAR.

And the Tripod, rather than immediately beginning the fight, turns its head slightly and emits an inhuman cry, a MECHANICAL BELLOW that rips over the landscape and echoes all the way across the river and washes back off the opposite bank:

"ULLA!"

80   ON THE DOCK,   80

the crowd surges forward onto the boat. Ray, holding Rachel, winces in pain as he tries to keep her from being crushed.

Rachel begins to panic, and Ray makes a space around her with his arms, the way Robbie did in the car.

                              RAY
                    This is your space, you hear me?! This
                    is your space, nobody's coming in here,
                    I will protect you!

Robbie, caught in the crush of people, actually loses touch with the ground, his feet lift right up off the decking and he moves forward as part of a massive organism, no control at all.

He SCREAMS for his father, Ray SCREAMS back, but there's nothing they can do to stay near each other, they're lost in the flood.

81   IN THE RIVER,   81

the massive propellers of the ferry boat CHURN the water as they start to turn, but they're digging too hard in an area that's too shallow, and they throw up an enormous spray of mud and silt that flies everywhere.

The boat lurches forward, throwing up a huge rooster tail of river mud.

The rear ramp of the ferry boat starts to rise up, spilling whoever was on it into the boat, and blocking the way for whoever was still on the dock.

People leap off the edge of the dock, grabbing onto the lip of the
rising ramp.

82   ON THE FERRY BOAT,   82

the still-tied aft ropes on the boat pull tight, and with a
horrible GROANING they rip the pilings out of the riverbed.

The massive boat moves out fast, a dozen people clinging to the
half-raised rear ramp, suspended over the churning propellers.

Robbie leaps forward, onto the roof of the rearmost car, and gets
himself up near the top of the ramp. He hauls people onboard, one
after another. Some slip and fall into the freezing river below,
but Robbie saves easily a half dozen.

Ray, nearby, is clutching Rachel, fighting to keep space around
her so she isn't crushed by the crowd. He watches Robbie,
impressed.

83   ON THE EMBANKMENT,   83

the Tripod that appeared from the forest remains at its edge, and
for a split-second it seems the boat may escape it simply by
virtue of being on the water. But then --

84   ON THE FERRY BOAT,   84

-- the boat, now fifty yards out into the river, lurches from a
sudden shift in the water beneath them.

Ray turns and looks over the side. The river is churning,
something's coming *up* from the river bottom, and as he looks --

-- *THE HEAD OF A TRIPOD BREAKS THE RIVER SURFACE.*

Everyone on board SCREAMS and the ferry boat tilts sharply to the
side, unbalanced by the sudden depression in the water.

The Tripod rises, higher and higher.

The deck of the ferry is at a thirty degree angle now, cars begin
to slide, tumbling toward the railing.

Ray grabs hold of Robbie, who's still working to help people on
board the boat.

                              ROBBIE
            HEY!

84   CONTINUED: 84

        But Ray doesn't have time to discuss it, cars are SLAMMING into
        the railing all around them now, he hurls Robbie over the side of
        the boat, away from the falling cars, then grabs hold of Rachel
        and jumps overboard himself.

        Just in time, too, because just the boat lurches again and half a
        dozen cars SMASH through the railing where they were standing.

84A-94   OMITTED   84A-94

95   UNDERWATER,   95

        Ray, Rachel, and Robbie are underwater, just starting to swim for
        the top. All around them, cars PLUNGE into the river, landing
        like depth charges and sinking immediately, their terrified
        OCCUPANTS pounding on the windows and trying like hell to open
        the doors.

        Ray and the kids kick for the surface --

95A   IN THE RIVER,   95A

        -- and find themselves just a few feet away from the churning
        propellers of the sinking ferry boat, which is slowly rolling
        over onto its top, its lights flickering as it hits the water.

        As the ferry boat twists in the water, they kick like hell to get
        away from the spinning blades.

        The boat itself, which is now half sunk and well on its way to
        going completely underwater, is churning the river like crazy,
        its lights still burning in the murky depths. They're buffeted
        beyond their control, sucked --

95B   UNDERWATER.   95B

        Beneath the surface, Ray, Robbie and Rachel tumble close to the
        massive propellers. The blades narrowly miss them, they kick for
        the top --

96   EXT   IN THE RIVER   NIGHT   96

        -- and again, their three heads break the surface.

        Ray GASPS, treading water hard. The other two are stunned, but
        alive, spitting river water.

        They turn and look back. The Tripod that's risen up from the
        middle of the river calls out -- *"ULLA!"*

        A moment later there's another mechanical sound, seemingly coming
        in response, and *TWO MORE TRIPODS* stride out of the forest,
        headed for the river.

96A ON TOP OF THE SINKING BOAT,   96A

a MAN teeters for balance, one of the last left behind. Suddenly
black snakelike tentacles wrap around his mid-section. He looks
down in horror --

-- and is swept up into the air. Following him, we look up and
see that the tentacles have come from underneath the Tripod
that's standing in the river.

The Man is swept aloft, and around behind the Tripod, which is
where we lose sight of him. We're unsure where he's going or what
it wants with him.

96B IN THE RIVER,   96B

the current is strong, it grabs hold of Ray and the kids and
sweeps them away from the sinking ferry boat, out into the middle
of the river. They GASP and struggle in the current.

Ray looks back, over his shoulder, at the ruins of the dock,
where the lead Tripod now unfurls its heat-ray and trains it on
the sinking ferry boat and the hundreds of innocent people
swarming on and around it.

The Tripod points the disk at the dock and there is a flash, a
silent brightness like summer lightning. Waves like rippling
heat distort the air between the Tripod and the dock, then --

                              RAY
                GO UNDER!

-- the three of them gulp air and kick down under the surface.

97 UNDERWATER,   97

we see the explosion of flame that means the ferry boat has been
incinerated. It's muffled under here, and seen through the prism
of dark river water, but still horrifying.

98 ABOVE THE SURFACE,   98

they bob up again, beyond the ferry boat now, pulled hard by the
river's current, more than halfway across.

The Tripods move forward into the river, their swarms of
tentacles pluck SCREAMING PASSENGERS right off the deck of the
burning, sinking boat. Where they go after they're swept up into
the air, we still can't see.

Ray and the kids continue to be swept downstream, just away from
the chaos, which is good because --

98   CONTINUED: 98

        -- the Tripods fire again. The heat-rays sweep in unison across
        the center of the river, directly into the swarm of SCREAMING
        innocents.

        A gigantic cloud of steam rises up from the touch of the heat-ray
        on the river. Strange objects start leaping out of the water and
        into the air, flopping all around Ray and the kids. They're
        fish.

        And if we wonder why they're leaping, we quickly put it together
        as the river around Ray and the kids ROILS, seven to eight foot
        waves wash toward them, and a huge cloud of steam washes over
        them, obscuring all their vision.

                              ROBBIE
                    THE WATER!

                              RACHEL
                    IT'S BURNING ME!

                              RAY
                    SWIM FOR SHORE!

        And they do, Ray grabbing Rachel and digging at the water with
        everything he's got.

        Behind them, the vast cloud of steam still blocks much of the
        destruction behind, but they can hear SCREAMS, hear the HISSING
        and BOILING of the water, and see the FLASHES of the heat-ray as
        it's applied again and again.

        They're near the shore now, but a huge, bubbling wave of water is
        washing straight towards them. The shore's just twenty feet
        away, then ten, but the boiling wave is just behind them too, the
        water rises up --

        -- they hurl themselves onto the river bank --

99   EXT   FAR RIVERBANK   NIGHT   99

        -- and the tide of *boiling water* erupts in front of them, just
        inches from their safe perch.

        They lie there for a moment, scalded, catching their breath. But
        with the SOUNDS of the destruction in the river --

                              RAY
                    Keep moving!

        -- he drags the kids to their feet and they begin to climb the far
        bank, towards higher ground.

100   EXT   ON THE HILLSIDE   NIGHT   100

Ray drags the kids upward, upward, two hundred yards, to the
brink of the embankment on the far side of the river from the
dock.

Finally, they collapse to the ground and look down at the
wholesale slaughter they so narrowly escaped.

It's a view of staggering destruction, and the first wide shot of
the mayhem that we've seen so far.

Through clouds of steam and billowing smoke, we see it all -- the
flaming dock (the boat has sunk by now), the drowning victims,
and the hideous Tripods, wading methodically through the river,
directing the heat-ray at any survivors as they make their way
upstream.

Raising his gaze, Ray looks up to the highlands, where TEN
THOUSAND REFUGEES are still flooding down the main road that
leads to the ferry dock, funneled directly into the massacre by
half a dozen Tripods that stalk behind them, spreading
destruction.

On the horizon beyond, fires dot the landscape as far as Ray can
see, and to the north, an even worse omen --

-- the sky is alive with yet another lightning storm, which will
birth more of these murdering machines. It's the rout of
civilization... the massacre of mankind.

Ray pulls his two children close, their burned, soaking bodies
huddled next to his, quivering with fear, but still alive.

                                                  CUT TO:

101-104   OMITTED   101-104

105   EXT   ANOTHER ROAD   NIGHT   105

Ray, Rachel, and Robbie trudge along another road, still no
people in sight. They're tired, been walking all night. Far up
ahead, they can see a remote old Victorian house near a hilltop.

SHRIEK!

The three of them nearly leap out of their shoes at a DEAFENING
SOUND. Instinctively, Ray and Rachel duck, just as --

-- *FOUR FIGHTER JETS SCREAM OVERHEAD.*

For the record, they're A10 Thunderbolt Warthogs, and we've never
seen fighters this low to the ground, they can't be more than a
hundred feet up.

They sweep over the ground, bank up slightly at the hilltop, and
swoop over the rise, disappearing down low on the other side.

Brilliant flashes of light follow moments later, lighting up the
gathering night, and hollow BOOMS come a few seconds later.

Robbie, who has stayed on his feet, lets out a WAR WHOOP and takes
off running in the direction the fighters went.

                         RAY
               Robbie!

He takes off after him, dragging Rachel by the hand.

And they're not alone -- a group of SIX OR SEVEN COLLEGE-AGE KIDS
emerge from the tree line to the east, following the path the
jets took, waving their arms in the air.

Ray notices them, looks around more as he runs toward the
hilltop. A FAMILY OF FOUR now emerges from the back of a van that
was nose-down in the ditch on the side of the road, it had looked
empty and abandoned but was really a hiding place.

And there's more -- from the old Victorian house on the eastern
horizon, a BURLY MAN of about fifty comes cautiously outside,
clutching a rifle, head darting from side to side.

The countryside, which seemed so abandoned a few minutes ago, is
suddenly alive with survivors coming out of hiding.

Ahead, Robbie races toward the hilltop, a couple hundred yards
ahead, rimmed by tall grass. Ray keeps moving after him, one
hand holding onto Rachel's arm firmly.

                         RAY (cont'd)
               Stop where you are! Stay together!

                         RACHEL
               Don't make me go closer! Don't make me
               look! I don't want to look!

                         RAY
               STAY TOGETHER!

Ahead, Robbie ducks suddenly as a brilliant flash lights up the
entire area like broad daylight. A split-second later, a bone
rattling EXPLOSION follows.

It's hard to describe just how loud the explosion is, but its
result is powerful. Ray and Rachel fall to their knees, hands
clamped over their ears.

Rachel SHOUTS something at Ray, but he can't hear her over the
still-echoing blast. He SHOUTS something back, same story.

He grabs hold of her again and pulls her up the hill, she's
SHOUTING her objections, but Robbie's still moving ahead of them,
crawling toward the top of the hill.

                         RAY (cont'd)
                I'm gonna get Robbie and be right back!
                Stay here, STAY RIGHT HERE!

Rachel nods frantically and digs herself into the hillside, hands
plastered over her ears, eyes screwed shut.

106   EXT   HILLTOP   NIGHT   106

Ray crawls toward the top of the rise as fast as he can, closing
in on Robbie, who is headed for a GROUP OF SOLDIERS who are
crouched at the rim of the hill, staring down into the valley
below. The noise up here is deafening, two of the Soldiers are
watching the battle below through binoculars, two more SHOUT into
radios, but we can't hear a word they're saying.

It's a command post up on the ridge, the Soldiers are using laser
targeting (for the fighter jets) and reconnaissance gear.

The battle itself is obscured by the tall waving grass, a thick
gray smoke that billows in over everything, and blinding flashes
that accompany the constant explosions coming from below.

Ray reaches the still-moving Robbie and hurls himself at him,
tackling him ten feet short of the top of the hill. He crashes to
the ground on top of him as the four fighter jets that flew
overhead earlier circle back for a strafing run, coming in low.

As the fighting rages between the Army and the invaders, another
battle rages between Ray and Robbie, as Ray SHOUTS in Robbie's
ear, pleading with him not to go over the hill. Robbie twists and
thrashes in response, trying to escape his father.

We can't hear anything they say, as MORTARS are exploding,
there's dense GUNFIRE, SHOUTING and SCREAMING from the battle
raging over the hilltop. (For suggested Ray speech, see APPENDIX
D.)

The entire hilltop goes white again, all the air in the valley
seems to suck inward in one concussive second, and then it's
exploded in another deafening KA-BOOM.

106   CONTINUED: 106

TWO PLATOONS of Marines pour over the ridge around them, down to
join the battle on the ground. Several CIVILIAN ONLOOKERS race
forward too, over the hillside, but any available Soldiers try to
deter them, to guide the civilians out of harm's way and to
safety.

Robbie rolls over and twists his foot free, but Ray lunges and
gets his arms wrapped around his son's midsection. The kid is
fighting him, trying like hell to wrench free.

As they struggle, Ray cranes his head to get a look down the hill,
back the way he came, to make sure Rachel is still there.

She's fifty feet below them, hands clamped over her ears,
SCREAMING, terrified, and there are TWO SWARMS OF SOLDIERS now
pounding their way up the hill, boots SLAMMING into the ground
all around her.

A WELL-MEANING FAMILY has a hold of her, they're pulling on her,
but she's resisting. Bodies cross in front of him, he loses
sight of her.

107   FURTHER DOWN THE HILL,   107

the Family, which must think Rachel is abandoned, is trying like
hell to get her to come with them.

                         RACHEL
             HE'S COMING BACK FOR ME! HE'S COMING
             BACK FOR ME!

108   ON THE HILLTOP,   108

Ray sees what's happening, he SHOUTS for her.

                         RAY
             RACHEL! RACHEL!

                         ROBBIE
             LET *GO* OF ME!

He swings a leg around and KICKS at his father, trying to get
free.

Below, Ray gets another glimpse of Rachel, she's calling out for
him, but she doesn't know where he is and the Well-Meaning Family
has a hold of her and they're dragging her off *in the opposite
direction*.

Ray looks back, to Robbie, who's now wriggling out of his grasp,
he's passing right through Ray's arms. Ray looks back down at
Rachel, SCREAMING for him as she's swept away, now passing
completely out of his line of sight.

Robbie's passing through his grasp, now just his feet are within reach, and Ray's got a hold of them, but knows what he has to do.

He lets go.

Ray and Robbie take off in opposite directions, Robbie throwing one last look back over his shoulder at his father as he dashes over the hillside the other way, headed down into the valley to join the attacking soldiers.

Ray races toward Rachel, fighting against the tide of Onlookers and Soldiers headed toward the hilltop.

109   FURTHER DOWN THE HILL,   109

Ray plows through a break in the people and he sees Rachel, being dragged away by the Well-Meaning Family. Ray's on her a second later, scooping her up into his arms.

                         RACHEL
          DADDY!

                         WELL-MEANING FATHER
          I'm sorry, we thought-

Ray's got no time for niceties, he ignores the family and whirls, looks back up at the hilltop.

                         RAY
          ROBBIE!

Night abruptly FLASHES into day again, and we know what this means, there's another one of those BLASTS coming. Ray and Rachel both instinctively clap their hands over their ears and here it comes again --

-- KA-BOOM!

Ray and Rachel pull their palms away from their ears, their hands slick with their own blood this time.

Ray SCREAMS for Robbie a few times more, open-mouthed, desperate, but we can't hear it.

Then, suddenly, the ROARING battle sounds fade, and there's only a strange silence coming from the valley.

Ray puts Rachel down, takes her by the hand again, and they look at each other, excited. Is it possible?

But just as hope rises --

-- a BURNING MAN races back over the hill and crashes into him.

Ray tackles the Burning Man and rolls him on the ground, gets the
flames out. He looks back up toward the hilltop --

-- as *HALF A DOZEN BURNING ONLOOKERS pour back over the hilltop!*

Ray moves as fast and as hard as he can, knocking them to the
ground, rolling them in the dirt. Now sound comes back, and with
a vengeance. HORRIBLE SCREAMS, explosions of flame.

Ray looks up, toward the top of the hill.

                         RAY (cont'd)
              ROBBIE! ROBBIE?!

Now military vehicles come pouring over the hilltop, headed back
this way, fast, and then soldiers on foot, running for their
lives in a massive, chaotic retreat.

And then, in pursuit -- *THE TOPS OF THREE TRIPODS* appear over the
crest of the hill.

Ray and Rachel freeze in momentary panic, just as the FOUR
FIGHTER JETS reappear, SCREAMING over the horizon to save the
day.

Ray and Rachel duck down, hands over their heads, and through the
blowing weeds, Ray sees four small projectiles HISS from beneath
the planes' wings.

The missiles head straight for the Tripods, but when they're a
good fifty yards away, the missiles explode harmlessly in midair, as if detonated by an invisible, protective shield around
the invading machines.

Ray and Rachel, fleeing, fall into an observation point, next to
TWO FORWARD AIR CONTROLLERS who are frantically trying to
redirect aircraft. A THIRD SOLDIER, an officer, leaps into the
pit, running back from the other side of the hill, burned and
streaked with dirt and blood. He grabs hold of the other
Soldiers, tries to drag them out of the pit.

                         SOLDIER 3
              Fall back! Move the hell back! Fall
              back five hundred meters on my ten
              o'clock!

                         SOLDIER 1
              Sir, we've dumped HE and sabot on these
              things, what have we got left? Tows?!
              Should we try the tows?!

> SOLDIER 3
> Doesn't matter what you fire, you can't
> get through, nothing punches through!

> SOLDIER 2
> What is it, some kind of shield?!

> SOLDIER 3
> (nods)
> We can't penetrate it, everything
> detonates before it even gets close!

Ray's heard enough. He grabs hold of Rachel and they crawl out of
the pit and run in the opposite direction, down the hill.

They near the bottom of the hill, still nowhere to go but
forward, ahead, away, but that won't do, they won't survive, and
just before panic hits --

> VOICE (O.S.)
> OVER HERE! *OVER HERE!*

-- he hears a VOICE and whirls. The Burly Man, the one they saw
coming out of the old Victorian house with a rifle before, is
fifty yards to the left, gesturing wildly to them.

Ray and Rachel change course and head toward him, running as fast
as their legs will carry them.

The Burly Man turns and takes off, waving them to follow, and
they do, toward the house, just beyond a stand of trees.

110-115 OMITTED   110-115

116   EXT   OLD HOUSE   NIGHT   116

The ROAR of the battle is still deafening as Ray and Rachel tear
across the front lawn of the old house, following the Burly Man.
He doesn't go in the front door, but instead to the side of the
house, where he throws open a storm cellar door.

117   INT   OLD HOUSE - CELLAR   NIGHT   117

Ray and Rachel stumble down the half flight of stairs and fall
into the cellar, GASPING for air.

The Burly Man drops his gun and goes to work on the storm cellar
doors, SLAMMING them shut and sliding a number of heavy bars and
locks into place to seal them.

He hurries down the stairs, out of breath himself, and squats in
front of them. The place is lit by a single hurricane lamp on top
of a red cooler.

117   CONTINUED:

                          BURLY MAN
                     You all right?

Rachel nods, unable to speak. Ray doesn't answer. The Burly Man
puts an arm on his shoulder.

                          BURLY MAN (cont'd)
                     What about you?

Ray just looks at him, unable to speak, his eyes big and empty.

                                                    CUT TO:

118   INT   OLD HOUSE - CELLAR   NIGHT   118

Later that night, maybe the middle of the night. The cellar is
lit only by the tiny flame enduring in the hurricane lamp.

On one side, there's a small cot, and Rachel is lying on it, under
a couple blankets. Ray's crouching beside it, stroking her hair
gently, WHISPERING to her. Her eyes are heavy, they want to be
closed, but she's trying like hell to keep them open. They're in
the middle of a conversation.

                          RACHEL
                     What do you mean? He got a ride? From
                     who?

                          RAY
                     Shhh, close your eyes.

                          RACHEL
                     With the army men?

                          RAY
                     He's... he's gonna meet us, honey. In
                     Boston. At Mom's. Close your eyes. Let
                     'em close. I'm right here...

She forces her eyes open again, WHISPERS to him.

                          RACHEL
                     Where do you think Mom is right this
                     minute?

                          RAY
                     Waiting for us. I think she and Tim are
                     in Boston at Grandma's house, and
                     they're all waiting for us.

                          RACHEL
                     Are you sure?

> RAY
> I think they can't sleep, because
> they're so worried about us, so they're
> sitting in the kitchen, and they're
> drinking that awful tea Grandma makes,
> and they're counting every minute until
> they see us again.

He reaches down to give her hand a squeeze, notices she's
clutching something there. It's a yellow third-place ribbon, the
one she tried to get him to notice earlier. She'd stuffed it in
her pocket.

Ray opens her fingers, pulls the ribbon out.

> RAY (cont'd)
> This yours? Did you win this?

> RACHEL
> (nods sleepily)
> I won third place.

> RAY
> It's beautiful. What'd you win it for?

> RACHEL
> (yawning)
> Walk, trot and canter. They call it
> hunter-jumper.

> RAY
> Well, I'm very impressed. I'm... I'm
> proud of you.

That's what you say to a kid in these circumstances, right?
Rachel smiles, starts to reply --

> RACHEL
> Sing me Lullaby & Goodnight.

> RAY
> I don't know that one.

> RACHEL
> Sing me Hushabye Mountain.

> RAY
> I don't know that one either.

She turns her head away, disappointed. Ray thinks for a moment,
then starts to sing softly, huskily. It's "Little Deuce Coupe,"
the Beach Boys song.

After a few lines, Rachel is asleep. Ray furrows his brow
slightly, that was odd, how quickly she fell asleep, but he puts
one hand on her stomach -- she's still breathing.

He pulls the blanket up around her chin and crosses the basement.
The Burly Man is sitting on a small folding camp chair next to the
cooler, the rifle over his knees. He gestures to another chair,
which he has unfolded for Ray.

Ray sits heavily, close to collapse, and drops his head in his
hands. The Burly Man reaches out and nudges him with the back of
one hand and Ray looks up -- he's offering a glass half-filled
with a clear liquid.

                         BURLY MAN
             Peach schnapps. Disgusting, I know.
             Found a whole case of this shit.

                         RAY
             Thank you.

Ray takes a sip. The Burly Man nods, knocks his back. He
breathes heavily, labored most of the time, maybe he's asthmatic.

                         BURLY MAN
             I'm sorry about your son.

Ray nods. They drink in silence for a moment. Then:

                         RAY
             Did you... lose anyone?

                         BURLY MAN
             All of 'em.

He looks away. That seems to be all he's going to say about that.
Ray respects it. The Burly Man holds out a hand.

                         BURLY MAN (cont'd)
             Harlan Ogilvy.

                         RAY
             Ray Ferrier.

They shake. Ogilvy offers a metal plate with some sliced ham and
bread on it. Ray takes some and eats.

                         RAY (cont'd)
             This your house?

                         OGILVY
             Found it empty.

He looks at Ray, but when Ray meets his eye, he fidgets. Maybe he
didn't find it empty.

                         OGILVY (cont'd)
              What?

                         RAY
              Didn't say a word.

Ray's eyes drop down, and for the first time he notices the large
hunting knife Ogilvy wears strapped to his ankle.

                         OGILVY
              Got water, food enough for weeks.
              You're welcome to stay. Both of you.

                         RAY
              Thank you. I gotta sleep...

He stands up.

                         OGILVY
              Those machines, those Tripods they
              got...

Ray turns back. Ogilvy shakes his head in dire admiration.

                         OGILVY (cont'd)
              Buried 'em right under our feet. Since
              before the first people were here.
              They've been planning this for a million
              years. We're beat to shit.

                         RAY
              Please keep your voice down.

                         OGILVY
              Think about it, they defeated the
              greatest power in the world in a couple
              days. Walked right over us. And these
              are only the first, they'll keep coming.
              This isn't a war, any more than there's
              a war between men and maggots.

                         RAY
              Then what is it?

                         OGILVY
              It's an extermination.

He pours himself some more schnapps. Ray nods. Again, he tries
to walk away. Again, Ogilvy won't let him.

> OGILVY (cont'd)
> You afraid?

> RAY
> Of course I'm afraid.

> OGILVY
> I've been around death plenty. Drive an
> ambulance in the city. *Drove* an
> ambulance. That's all over now.

> RAY
> New York?

> OGILVY
> You know the people that make it? The
> ones that don't flatline before the
> hospital? It's the ones that keep their
> eyes open, that keep looking at you,
> keep *thinking*, they're the ones who
> survive. We can't lose our heads, Ray.
> Running, that's what'll kill you. And
> I'm dead set on living.
>   (laughs bitterly)
> "Dead set on living."

He finishes his schnapps again and pours himself some more. Ray
watches him. This is starting to be a concern.

Somewhere far off in the distance, there is a hollow BOOM.

> RAY
> Thank you for taking us in.

Ray goes to the other side of the basement, where Rachel is
asleep. He lies down on the floor next to her cot, makes a pillow
of his jacket.

More hollow BOOMS, except they're slightly closer.

Ogilvy, still sitting with his back to him and faintly
silhouetted by the hurricane lamp, calls out in a normal, too-
loud voice.

> OGILVY
> Not gonna be exterminated!

Ray closes his eyes, but a few chunks of earth and plaster fall
from the ceiling and land on the floor around him.

He opens his eyes. More debris wafts down onto his face. Ray
sits up and looks over at Ogilvy, who turns around to face him, a
mad grin on his face.

118 CONTINUED: (5)   118

                              OGILVY (cont'd)
                    We're gonna fight 'em, Ray. They gotta
                    have a weakness. Somehow they killed a
                    few of those things in Osaka, that's
                    what I heard. You telling me the Japs
                    can figure it out but we can't?

He comes over and elbows Ray in the ribs, a hard, macho gesture.
Ray GROANS in pain, his ribs are probably fractured.

From just outside, a loud, rhythmic POUNDING begins, like the
sound of a factory coming back to life after lunch hour. The
house above them SHUDDERS. Ray gets to his feet, a horrible
thought growing in his mind.

                              OGILVY (cont'd)
                    It's okay.

He leans forward, opens the door on the hurricane lamp, and PUFFS
out the flame, plunging the basement into near-darkness.

                              OGILVY (cont'd)
                    Have a look.

He stands, still clutching the rifle, and scurries across the
room, gesturing to Ray to follow. He climbs up on an overturned
crate, onto a small ledge built into the wall.

When he climbs on it, his face is right at window level. A board
has been cut to fit the window space and slid into place, now
Ogilvy slides it back slightly so he can see outside.

Putting a finger to his lips, a signal to Ray to keep quiet, he
hops off the wall and gestures to Ray to climb up.

Ray does, with dread. Ogilvy gestures -- look through the slit.

119 THROUGH THE SLIT,   119

Ray can see the open area to the side of the house. But it isn't
open field any more.

TWO TRIPODS have made their encampment in the field, and as Ray
watches a THIRD TRIPOD strides out from the trees, calling to the
others in its familiar mechanical tone.

"ULLA!"

120 IN THE CELLAR,   120

Ray's face snaps away from the window in horror. Ogilvy, who
seemed to know about this, seems unconcerned.

120   CONTINUED:

                              OGILVY
                    Don't worry, they can't hear us when
                    those things are on.

He scurries across the basement, climbs a ladder on the other
side, and pushes aside another piece of plywood that he's used to
obscure the window over there.

Again, he gestures to Ray, who races silently across the room and
up the ladder.

121   THROUGH THE SECOND SLIT,   121

Ray sees ANOTHER TRIPOD on this side of the house, and as he
watches its GIANT MECHANICAL LEGS stride right past the window
and stop.

With an otherworldly GROAN, the legs contract into themselves,
lowering the "head" of the Tripod down to ground level.

There's a FLASH of brilliant light from within the head of the
Tripod that momentarily illuminates the fields around the house,
and in that flash we see equipment, dug-out pits, a bivouac --
clear evidence that this is, and has been, an alien encampment.

In their hurry to get inside, Ray and Rachel didn't notice it all
before, but they are now living in a house taken over.

122   BACK IN THE BASEMENT,   122

Ray leaps off the ladder and lands in front of Ogilvy, who's
pleased at showing off the true nature of their location. Ray
grabs him by the shirt, drags his face right up to his.

                              RAY
                    You *knew?!* Are you *insane?!* How could
                    you bring us here?!

                              OGILVY
                    So we could fight 'em together, Ray!
                    Now *we're* the ones coming up from
                    underground. And when the time's right,
                    we'll take them by surprise, the way
                    they took us.

Ray looks at him, realizing too late this guy's lost it.

                              OGILVY (cont'd)
                    Right under their feet, Ray. Right here
                    under their feet.

122 CONTINUED: 122

                              RAY
                 You killed us. You just killed us.

                                                      CUT TO:

123 EXT   OLD HOUSE   DAY   123

     The next morning.

     SFFFT! A piece of plywood slides away and an eyeball appears
     right in front of us. We're outside the old house, down at ground
     level.

     There's something strange about the landscape out here,
     everywhere there is dirt or grass or moisture, there is a
     creeping red fuzz, a red weed. We've seen these clawing tendrils
     before, on the surface of the barren planet in the opening.

     The red weed seethes, swarming over a dripping outdoor faucet at
     the base of the house.

     Ray's eye is peering out through the basement slit, looking
     furtively from side to side. The sounds of HEAVY MACHINERY can
     be heard behind us, the rhythmic, pounding drone of a factory.
     The shadows of tall, moving shapes play across the house.

124 INT   OLD HOUSE - CELLAR   DAY   124

     Ray slides the piece of wood back into place and hops off the
     narrow ledge. He's upset, didn't like what he saw, clearly
     they're still hemmed in by the Tripods. The POUNDING MACHINERY
     is deep and penetrating here in the basement, and it will hammer
     away constantly the entire time they're here.

     Up near the window, he sees the tendrils of a batch of red weed
     growing around the edge of the window, making their way into the
     basement.

     He reaches up and RIPS them off. They're tough, sinewy, it takes
     a few pulls.

     He looks across the room, sees Rachel still asleep on the cot.

     Ogilvy is back on the camp chair, his rifle across his legs,
     rocking back and forth slightly, watching Ray's every move.

                                                      CUT TO:

124A INT   CELLAR - A SHORT TIME LATER   DAY   124A

     Later. Ray is beside Rachel's cot. She's awake now, and looking
     up at him apprehensively.

With a dull SCRAPE, he strikes a match from a book of matches. He
holds a straight pin in the other hand and passes it back and
forth through the flame, sterilizing it. Rachel stares at him
with wide, teary eyes, fixed on the pin. She's got her left hand
balled up in a fist and is clutching it to herself.

                         RAY
                    (whispering)
               It's infected. It's got to come out or
               it'll just get worse.

Reluctantly, Rachel opens her hand and we get a look at her palm --
the sliver she got a few days ago is indeed infected, the skin is
puffy, red and angry all around it. Ray moves the pin closer.

                         RACHEL
               Do you have to do that?

Ray puts down the pin, reaches down carefully, and pinches the
end of the protruding splinter.

                         RAY
               Not anymore. Look, the infection pushed
               it out a little.

He pulls it the rest of the way out and Rachel snatches her hand
back happily.

                         RACHEL
               Told you. It wasn't supposed to be
               there, so my body got rid of it.

                         RAY
               Yeah. It did, didn't it.

                         RACHEL
                    (pause, then)
               How long are we going to stay here?

                         RAY
               Not long. We need to wait for the right
               moment, and then we're going to leave
               and find another place to stay.

                         RACHEL
               Are we still going to Mom's?

                         RAY
               Of course we are. But in the meantime,
               just try not to make a sound and I'll
               bring you something to eat and drink,
               okay?

Rachel nods, fearful. Ray nods back, good for you, and turns to get some food. But Ogilvy is right behind him.

>   OGILVY
>   Leave? What's the matter with you,
>   we're gonna *fight*. I already started a
>   tunnel, you wanna see it?

>   RAY
>   No, I don't want to see your tunnel.

He goes across the room to the other slit and slides it open. Nothing encouraging there either. More red weed drips down the wall here, Ray rips that off too.

>   OGILVY
>   What we've got to do is get to the
>   cities. We'll have our own tunnels
>   there, ready-made. The *subways*, see
>   what I'm saying?

>   RAY
>   Keep your voice down.

>   OGILVY
>   We can hide a whole army down there.
>   We'll go underground, stage attacks at
>   night. We're the Resistance, Ray. They
>   can't occupy this country, occupations
>   always fail, history taught us that a
>   thousand times. This is *our land,* we
>   eat it, we breathe it, only we can live
>   on it. They can't survive here, they
>   weren't built for it, they-

Ray swerves over in front of him and bends down, holding a finger up in front of Ogilvy's face. He speaks in a whisper (as he will the whole time they're in the cellar).

>   RAY
>   Keep. Your voice. *Down.*

Ogilvy stares right back at him, with meaning. Ray looks down. The barrel of Ogilvy's gun is pointed at him. He pushes it away with one finger and leans in to Ogilvy's ear.

>   RAY (cont'd)
>   You know the first time you fire that,
>   we're all dead.

>   OGILVY
>   You don't know how well I shoot.

                              RAY
                    I don't *care* how well you shoot, they'll
                    hear it.

                              OGILVY
                    I told you, they can't hear us when
                    those things are pounding.

                              RAY
                    Just remember what I said.

Ogilvy stares at him.

And takes another swig of schnapps.

                                                      CUT TO:

125-125B OMITTED   125-125B

126 INT   CELLAR   NIGHT   126

Nighttime. Still in the cellar. The red weed Ray tore down has
grown back in from around the corners of the windows. The
rhythmic POUNDING goes on.

Water has pooled in the basement from a dripping spigot on the
far side. Rachel is huddled in a dry corner, her hands clamped
over her ears, going quietly insane from the constant noise.

Ogilvy comes over to her, slides down onto the floor next to her.
He's half drunk.

                              OGILVY
                    You miss your mommy?

Rachel just looks back at him, scared, doesn't answer. Ray, who
is across the cellar getting some food onto a plate for Rachel,
notices Ogilvy talking to her.

                              OGILVY (cont'd)
                    I had a girl nearly your age. If
                    anything happens to your daddy, I'll
                    take care of you.

Ray grabs Ogilvy by the collar and turns him away from Rachel,
but does so subtly, so his daughter doesn't notice the force
behind the gesture.

                              RAY
                        (low voice)
                    You've got nothing to say to her.
                    Understand?
                            (MORE)

                              RAY (cont'd)
                    You want to talk to somebody, you got a
                    question, you ask me.

Ogilvy looks at him, measures whether a fight with Ray is a good
or bad thing.

                              OGILVY
                    Yeah, I got a question. What exactly is
                    your *plan*, Ray? I mean, I know what I'm
                    gonna do, what about you? You gonna
                    just sit here, wait for them to come get
                    you? Is that it? Is that what you've
                    got up your sleeve?

He gets up and grabs his wheelbarrow, goes noisily across the
basement to go back to work.

                              RAY
                    Keep the noise down.`

                              OGILVY
                       (almost shouting)
                    Maybe you *want* to be caught... couple
                    days hiding in a basement, too much for
                    you, I bet.

                              RAY
                    Shut up!

Suddenly, the pounding stops. It's quiet out there now, VERY
quiet. As if they heard something.

                              RAY (cont'd)
                    Listen! It stopped.

But Ogilvy pays it no mind, he keeps talking in a normal voice.

                              OGILVY
                    Probably turn yourself right in, that's
                    what you'll do. Wonder what you ever
                    did before they came along and changed
                    your life.

Ray goes over in front of him, gets right in his face.

                              RAY
                    Listen! Shut up!

                              OGILVY
                    Maybe you'll be okay. Maybe you'll get
                    lucky, they'll take you as a pet.

                              RACHEL
                    Dad!

Ray turns, sees what Rachel is pointing at. At one of the slits,
there is movement, the plywood is being rattled.

                         OGILVY
                You know, feed you, throw a ball for you
                to fetch, get all sentimental over the
                pet boy they love so much until he the
                day he bites somebody and they have to
                put him down.

Abruptly, *the plywood flies off the slit*. Punched by something
from the other side, it breaks the glass as well, chunks of it
SMASH and CLATTER on the cellar floor.

They all freeze, dead silent, even Ogilvy, as *something* moves
through the window.

It's dark in here, lit only by the irregular light coming in from
outside, so it's hard to see much, but what it looks like is
something about the size of a football, but sharp-edged,
triangular, a glowing searchlight at its tip. It's a probe, the
kind they saw going into the suburban house earlier. The only
sound in the basement is the steady drip-drip-drip of the leaky
spigot in the far wall.

It slithers into the basement, looking around, almost like a
human head, turning from side to side, sliding alongside objects
like a cat, gathering data.

Ray looks at Ogilvy, to make sure he's still silent. He is, but
he's also looking up at the wall nearby them with intent. Ray
follows his gaze.

Ogilvy's looking at an axe that's hanging on the wall.

Ogilvy glances at Ray, looks back up at the axe, then back at Ray.
He mouths words, silently.

                         OGILVY (cont'd)
                    (I CAN GET IT!)

Ray understands, all right, but shakes his head no, vehemently.

The probe moves down to ground level and oozes across the floor,
searching, searching. It draws closer to them. Ray catches eyes
with Rachel, who's terrified, and mouths words to her --

                         RAY
                    (DO NOT MOVE.)

Just before it reaches them, the probe finds a door slightly ajar
(it leads to a root cellar) and it passes through there.

As soon as it's out of sight, Ogilvy straightens up to grab the
axe off the wall. Ray stands and grabs hold of his arm to stop
him, but Ogilvy swings an elbow into Ray's broken ribs, hard.

Ray crumples to the floor in pain, is dying to scream, but
manages to stifle it.

Ogilvy snatches the axe and crouches down again, raising it,
waiting for the probe to come back into the room.

From the floor, Ray looks around frantically and spots a large
old mirror leaning up against the wall nearby. In great pain, he
raises himself up on one elbow and crawls forward to it.

He grabs hold of the mirror's gilt edges and drags it slowly,
silently over in front of himself and Rachel. Ogilvy, nearby,
still has the axe raised in readiness.

Ray HISSES for his attention, imploring the man to come behind
the mirror. Ogilvy shakes his head no, but Ray mouths silently.

                    RAY (CONT'D)
          (NOT NOW. LATER. PLEASE. NOT NOW.)

Ogilvy debates, still leaving himself out in the open.

                    RAY (cont'd)
          (WE WILL GET THEM LATER. I PROMISE.)

The probe, perhaps hearing them, pulls out of the root cellar and
back into the main room, just as Ogilvy reluctantly decides to
scamper behind the mirror.

The probe senses the movement and darts quickly across the room,
bumping gently into the surface of the mirror.

Behind the mirror, Ray, Rachel, and Ogilvy all remain frozen.

The probe's head recoils from the mirror, seems to tilt its head
in curiosity. The mirror *fogs* right in front of it, maybe the
probe expels CO_2, like a breathing organism.

It studies the mirror for one more moment, then with a piercing
HISS, it's recalled, slithering back across the cellar at top
speed and whipping up and out through the now-broken window.

After a moment, the RHYTHMIC POUNDING of the machinery resumes.

Ray drags himself up into a sitting position, leaning against the
wall, nursing his ribs, Rachel at his side. Ogilvy sits cross-
legged, staring at him, still holding the axe.

> OGILVY
> I got my doubts about you, Mister.

Ray stares him down. He's about to get up and take Rachel back to the other side of the basement, but he freezes, staring down at the water that's pooled on the basement floor. There are ripples in it, little wavelets flowing toward him.

Reflexively, he hunches hunch down in the hiding place again, listening. The ripples get bigger, something is *moving* on the far side of the basement. Rachel looks up at Ray, her eyes pleading -- "what is it?" Ray shakes his head, "don't move."

They listen. Across the room, they can hear a LABORED BREATHING, thick, short, wet breaths. Non-human breaths.

Ray moves, *slowly*, raising his head to peer between some laundry that hangs from a clothesline overhead.

THROUGH THE LAUNDRY,

he gets his first (and only) good look at the rounded bulk of one of the *CREATURES*.

It's about five feet long, dense, sluglike in appearance. It has three stubby limbs, all underneath it, and a long set of tendrils around its "mouth," similar to the ones that dangle beneath the belly of the Tripod it's operating. Its skin is somewhat translucent, its internal organs visible through it.

Its "mouth" is shoved over the dripping water spigot on the far wall, SLURPING at the precious liquid. Its breathing is very heavy and slow, it seems ill or incapacitated in some way. As Ray watches *TWO MORE* of the things slither through the window opening, their body mass streamlining to get through the narrow space, then re-expanding as they land on the basement floor.

As the first creature sucks at the water pipe, the second goes to it, perhaps to check on it. The third creature rummages through the stuff on the basement floor, using its tendrils to dip into a cardboard box filled with photographs.

It scatters most of them across the basement floor, but finds one that might be of interest. It passes it over to the second creature, which takes it from it and examines it.

BEHIND THE HANGING LAUNDRY,

Ray holds his breath. Ogilvy, who is full of tough talk when not faced with danger, is frozen in abject horror. Rachel, thankfully, has her view obscured and can't see what's going on.

IN THE MIRROR,

the creatures just start to move across the basement, toward the
three humans crouched in the far corner, when -- *ULLA!* -- a
mechanical cry from the Tripod outside sounds. The three bulky
creatures move quickly and with sudden power, even nimble, their
stubby legs propelling them rapidly across the floor, up the
wall, and out the window, to rejoin their ship.

IN HIS HIDING PLACE,

Ray exhales deeply and turns around to face Rachel. He looks
down at his hands, which have been balled up into fists. He
forces himself to unclench. There are four red gashes in each
palm, where his nails dug into his skin in fear.

                                                      CUT TO:

127   INT   OLD HOUSE - CELLAR   DAY   127

The next day. Or maybe the one after that. They're blending
together now. One thing we know for sure -- there's a hell of a
lot more red weed in here than their used to be. It fringes the
windows, of course, but it's dripping down the walls too.

Ray, who's staring up at one of the windows, does a double take.
Through a gap in the frame, there's a thin red mist coming into
the basement, like gas seeping through the cracks.

Ogilvy's across the room, staring out one of the slits.

Ray stands and goes to window where the red mist is filtering in.
He holds out a hand. The red mist covers his hand and he pulls it
back, looks at it. Rubs his fingers together.

The red substance smears, and it looks and feels unpleasantly
familiar. Deep down, Ray probably knows what it is but doesn't
want to admit it.

He looks up at the wall, where the red mist has settled over a
patch of red weed, which is twitching and growing excitedly
underneath it.

Suddenly, from the other side of the room, Ogilvy emits a stunned
CRY (which he fails to mute) and falls backwards.

Ray leaps forward and catches him before he tumbles off the
narrow ledge, preventing the racket that would have come from him
hitting the floor.

                         RAY
               What is it?! What?

                       OGILVY
               The... that thing! It... it...

127 CONTINUED:

Ray scrambles up to the ledge and peers out through the slit.

128 THROUGH THE SLIT,   128

he sees the legs of one of the Tripods as it returns. This Tripod
has a different feature than we've seen before, a device that
extends from its shell, a large metallic basket of some sort,
affixed to its back.

Ray squints, trying to figure out this new development, but
Ogilvy's hands are on him, pulling at him, to get at the slit.

                         OGILVY
               Let me see!

Ray swats him away like a fly, looks back through the slit.

Suddenly, from the underbelly of the Tripod's "head," half a
dozen whiplike tendrils shoot out and extend to about a hundred
feet in length each.

They snake around, up to the basket on the back of the machine,
and slither inside it. *HUMAN SCREAMS* come from inside.

                         RAY
               Oh God...

The tendrils emerge from the basket, wrapped around the body of a
MAN IN HIS FORTIES. The Man is injured but still conscious,
SHRIEKING.

The tendrils snap, hurling the Man to the ground just behind a
large pile of dirt, then they stiffen, pinning him there, just
out of our sight.

The Tripod shifts so that it's standing directly over him, then a
thin pipette emerges from its base and shoots straight down, into
the earth where the man was screaming.

And he stops screaming.

The translucent pipette turns red as blood flows up through it.

Ray GASPS, staring in horror. Suddenly, from the back of the
Tripod, a thick red mist sprays out, covering the field of red
weed below.

129 BACK IN THE CELLAR,   129

Ray whips away from the slit, horrified, and looks again at the
red mist coming through the window on the far side, and at the red
smear on his hand.

129   CONTINUED:

It's blood, *human* blood, and they're using it to fertilize the
red weed.

Hands shaking, Ray finds the piece of plywood and slides it back
into place, obscuring the window.

He looks across the room and sees Rachel, who's staring at him,
desperate for information (right, like he's gonna tell her *this*).
Ogilvy is nowhere to be found.

But suddenly there's a sharp SCRAPING sound from across the
basement. Loud, *way* too loud.

Ray leaps off the ledge and hurries across the basement to the
small root cellar that's off to one side. He opens the door.

130   INT   ROOT CELLAR   DAY   130

Ogilvy is inside, standing waist deep in a hole, shovel in hand,
his asthmatic breathing louder than ever. He's digging like a
crazy man. This must be the "tunnel" he was so proud of.

                         RAY
          Stop it!

                         OGILVY
                    (WAY too loud)
          Christ, did you see it drinking?!

Ray grabs him by the arm roughly.

                         RAY
          Be quiet!

                         OGILVY
          They *drink* us!

He jams the shovel into the ground, it CLANGS off a rock.

                         RAY
          They'll hear you!

He reaches out to grab hold of the shovel, to pull it away from
Ogilvy, but the man swings it instead, catching Ray hard in the
side of the neck.

Ray GROANS and falls back. He rolls over, WHISPERING
desperately.

                         RAY (cont'd)
          Please, you've got to be quiet!

>   OGILVY
>   (loud)
>   Get to the city! Tunnel into the
>   subway!

>   RAY
>   I won't let my daughter die because of
>   you! Do you hear what I'm saying? Do
>   you understand?!

Ray gets up, to go to him again, but Ogilvy whirls, brandishing
the shovel.

>   OGILVY
>   Not MY blood!

Ray looks at him. Ogilvy has gone completely unhinged.

131   INT   OLD HOUSE - CELLAR   DAY   131

Ray comes out of the root cellar and into the basement, looking
around for something, searching, searching.

Rachel watches him, puzzled.

Outside, the SCREAMS and the CLANKING of machinery are louder
now, it's possible they haven't heard the sound of the digging in
the root cellar.

From the other room, Ogilvy can be heard ranting, LOUD.

>   RACHEL
>   (a whisper)
>   Dad?

Ray finds what he was looking for, or something close enough
anyway. It's an old tee shirt.

He goes to Rachel and drops to his knees in front of her.

>   RACHEL (cont'd)
>   What are you doing?

>   RAY
>   No matter what you hear, do not take
>   this off. Okay?

Rachel of course has no clue what he's talking about, but she
nods anyway.

Ray reaches out and wraps the tee shirt around her head, tying it
firmly in the back.

It's a blindfold.

Ray checks to make sure it's tight, then turns and hurries out of frame.

We stay on Rachel's face, half-covered by the dirty tee shirt, and see none of what follows, we only hear the sounds and see the reactions on Rachel's obscured face.

First we hear the digging, louder than ever, and Ogilvy's RANTING, coming from the other room, and his RASPY BREATHING, louder than ever. Then footsteps, silent, swift ones as they head toward him.

A door closes. Maybe the door to the root cellar? The digging stops. There are urgent, muffled sounds. More SHOUTING, Ogilvy again, much too loud.

Then a silence, a long one, punctuated occasionally by slight sounds of thrashing, and that breathing, still that RASPY BREATHING, but it's all off screen and through a closed door, and it's hard to tell.

A long moment goes by. Only silence.

And the BREATHING. Raspy, labored breathing. But only one person now.

A door CREAKS open. Then closes, very softly.

Footsteps again. Heavy BREATHING. Someone sliding to the floor.

Slowly, Rachel reaches up and pulls the blindfold from her eyes, terrified at what she'll see.

She blinks at the light. On the far side of the basement, she sees her father, slumped against the wall, a vacant expression on his face, breathing hard from the struggle. It was *his* breathing she heard.

He won't look at her.

Rachel turns toward the root cellar, sees the door hanging open a few inches. And no sounds coming from inside it.

She crawls across the floor of the basement silently, and curls up against her father. He puts one arm around her and pulls her tight, but can't look at her.

Softly, Rachel starts to speak, through tears:

                         RACHEL
              I want to show you my school. I want to
              show you where I sit, and my homework,
              and I want you to eat dinner at my house.
              I want you to pick me up from riding
              practice, I want you to meet my friend
              Paige, I want... I want you...

He reaches down, very gently, and wipes the tears from her
cheeks.

                         RAY
                    (whispers)
              You've got me.

We move in on his eyes, haunted, dark-circled, move all the way
in until they fill the frame, and then we dissolve to --

                                             DISSOLVE TO:

132   INT   OLD HOUSE - CELLAR   DAY   132

     -- the same eyes, but now we're pulling back, and we can tell time
has passed, it shows in the gauntness in their faces and the
beard growth on Ray's face. He and Rachel are in basically the
same position, still slumped against the wall.

Red weed is engulfing the basement, double the density it was
before. The area around Ray and Rachel looks like they've hacked
out a space in the jungle.

133   OMITTED   133

134   INT   OLD HOUSE - CELLAR   NIGHT   134

The same position, later still. It's nighttime. Both of them
are asleep, slumped against the wall. Close on Rachel's eyes as
they open. She blinks. Stares. Her eyes pop wide, but she
doesn't move, doesn't breathe, doesn't dare, because not twelve
inches away from her face --

-- IS AN ALIEN PROBE.

It's the same kind that slithered into the basement earlier, the
one they eluded, but this one seems to have come in while they
were sleeping, and there's no avoiding it this time.

Rachel lets out a tiny GASP of terror, which awakens Ray. He
jerks awake and sees the thing too, sucks his breath in hard, and
that moment of recognition convinces Rachel she's not dreaming.

CONTINUED:

She SCREAMS.

All the quiet that's been building in the cellar explodes in a
long, deafening SHRIEK as Rachel empties her lungs in terror.

The probe jerks back a foot or so, Ray tries to cover Rachel's
mouth, but this is it, she's snapping, she can't take it anymore.
Ray lunges for the axe that's nearby and attacks the probe,
swinging wildly, making some contact.

Rachel, beyond reason, scrambles to her feet and takes off, up
the stairs that lead into the house.

                         RAY
              Rachel!

But she's already gone, out of the basement, and Ray is delayed
by his battle with the probe. He lands a decisive blow and lops
the head off the thing, its remnant withdraws quickly, back and
out through the window it came in. Ray takes off after Rachel.

134A INT   OLD HOUSE - HALLWAY   NIGHT   134A

A door SMASHES open from the basement and Ray bursts out into the
darkened hallway of the old house they've been hiding under.

                         RAY
              RACHEL?!

But she's already gone, and the front door is hanging open. He
races after her, out the front door and into --

135-136   OMITTED   135-136

137   EXT   OLD HOUSE   NIGHT   137

   -- the weird and lurid landscape of another world.

Ray comes tearing down the front steps of the house and into the
yard beyond. Everywhere, in every direction, the red weed has
spread and multiplied, it's an ocean of crimson, it covers
everything in sight and extends as far as the eye can see.

                         RAY
              RACHEL!!!

But she's gone, he can't see her anywhere, and now he's in the
middle of the open area in front of the house, completely
exposed, and before he even has time to calculate the danger he's
in --

-- A TRIPOD LEG CRUNCHES DOWN IN FRONT OF HIM.

137   CONTINUED:

Ray freezes, utterly terrified, and looks up. The Tripod is
standing right over him, that enormous, humanoid "head" that
makes up its top is staring down at him. A flock of black crows
swarm around the head of the Tripod, and at this point we
understand why -- they're hoping for carrion.

Immediately, two grabbing tentacles swing down from the Tripod's
underbelly and WHIR through the air toward Ray.

Ray lunges into the nearest cover --

138   INT   PICKUP TRUCK   NIGHT   138

-- an old pickup truck parked nearby. He SLAMS the door and one
of the tentacles SMASHES through it, SNAPPING after him.

The second tentacle SMASHES through the passenger side window,
and now he's trapped, stuck between the two of them. Ray
flattens himself on the floor, as low as he can get, and the truck
suddenly jerks off the ground, lifted into the air by the
tentacles.

It sails through the air, turns over three times, and SMASHES
back down onto the ground, bouncing Ray off ceiling and floor
like a rag doll.

As soon as he can breathe he sits up, looks out through the
smashed windshield --

-- and sees Rachel. She's just standing there, about fifty yards
away, at the edge of the field of red weed, SCREAMING.

                         RAY
               RACHEL, GET DOWN, GET-

But the Tripod sees her too, and gives up its attack on Ray. It
turns and hits the gas, enormous legs covering the ground between
it and Rachel in a matter of seconds.

139   EXT   OLD HOUSE   NIGHT   139

Ray kicks open the twisted door of the pickup truck and takes off
across the open space, toward Rachel.

But the Tripod has a head start and is a hell of a lot faster. It
reaches her, and the next thing happens so fast it's hard to
comprehend -- the Tripod walks right over top of Rachel, four of
its whiplike tendrils wrap around her and lift her off the
ground.

Ray watches in shock as the tendrils rise up into the air and
deposit the still-screaming Rachel into the barred basket it
wears on its back.

139   CONTINUED:

Ray SCREAMS, but the Tripod's already moving away from him.

                              RAY
                RACHEL!!!

He looks around frantically for a weapon, anything at all. He
sees a Humvee, the burned-out military vehicle that rolled past
them earlier.

He races to it, rips the door open and searches through the
charred interior. He finds an automatic pistol and a grenade
belt. Those'll do.

140   EXT   THE MEADOW   NIGHT   140

Ray takes off into a vast field of red weed, chasing after the
Tripod. He can see it in the distance, moving quickly away from
him, covering huge chunks of ground.

He SCREAMS at it, trying to get its attention. He's just making
sounds, beyond words at this point.

He FIRES the automatic pistol, six, seven, eight shots, in the
distance we can see two or three of them TING off the surface of
the Tripod.

And it stops.

And it turns.

It's about three hundred yards away from Ray now, and this is it,
this is what it's all come down to, one human being against one
Tripod, and of course he doesn't stand a chance in hell.

                              RAY
                Come on... come on...

The Tripod stands there for a moment, evaluating him. The black
arm extends from its side, the heat-ray disc emerges.

                              RAY (cont'd)
                I'm right here...
                    (screaming)
                I'M NOT GOING ANYWHERE!   YOU HEAR ME?!
                COME AND GET ME, GOD DAMN IT, COME AND
                GET ME!!!

The Tripod seems to think about that for a second. And then the
disc rotates, flattens, and the arm retracts into the head of the
Tripod.

140   CONTINUED:

It starts to walk, normal speed at first and then fast, *really* fast, right toward him, its legs covering the couple hundred yards in an elegant, beautiful blur of motion.

Ray takes a breath, sucking in as much air as he can get. His whole body trembles, he tightens his grip on the belt of hand grenades, and he holds his ground.

The Tripod's close, fifty yards or less, the black tendrils whip out from the underbelly of its head, they drop down --

-- Ray forces his eyes to stay open, the shadow of the Tripod falls over him, the tendrils wrap around him --

-- *and he's swept off his feet!*

141-143   OMITTED   141-143

144   IN MIDAIR,   144

suddenly everything is moving. When we were in the meadow we had a wide-open view of events, but now we have almost *no* view of what's going on, so chaotic is the movement.

Ray is caught in the tendrils, being lifted up into the air, fast, upside-down now while the Tripod turns and takes off across the field again, headed God knows where.

Ray is hurled aloft, the tendrils release him, and he CRASHES down --

145   INT   ON BOARD THE TRIPOD   NIGHT   145

-- in the metallic basket on the Tripod's back. A series of "bars" close over the top of the basket, trapping him inside. It's noisy up here, the WHIRRING of the machinery very loud, the sound of the wind RUSHING past, and the SCREAMS --

-- of the other humans caught in the basket. Ray has landed face down on the floor of it, but when he rolls over he sees there are FIVE OTHER PEOPLE in the basket with him. More on them in a second.

The basket itself, which looked metallic when we saw it from down on the ground, is actually more biological in nature when you're up close, or in it. Though its surface glints in the sunlight, it seems to seethe, to move as the Tripod moves. And the "bars" are more like the slick limbs of jungle trees, dense as hell, but not brittle like metal.

The whole thing is maybe only eight feet square and three feet
high, so Ray, who has landed face down in it, is actually on *top*
of the other people inside, they're like corpses thrown into a
shallow pit, or lobsters in a pen, a pile of arms and legs and
writhing torsos.

Ray adjusts and finds himself face to face, seemingly with all of
them. There's an ARMY PRIVATE, a BUSINESSWOMAN, TWO TEENAGERS,
and an OLDER WOMAN.

                         RAY
              Rachel?! Rachel!

There's much SHOUTING back, people are twisting and turning,
trying to get off of each other to little avail, as the basket
bounces and shakes and rattles as the Tripod keeps moving.

Ray doesn't hear Rachel, but through the twisting bunch of
humanity he gets a glimpse of his little girl's face, trapped
beneath two others.

Ray reaches out a hand for her, she reaches back, through the
mass of people, but just when they're about to connect --

-- the basket tilts up at a forty-five degree angle suddenly,
producing a fresh round of SCREAMING from the trapped humans.

Ray is lying with his head on the lower end of the basket now, and
through his upside-down viewpoint, we see what's happening.

A small round opening, about eighteen inches across, irises open
at what is now the base of the basket. It's not a door, exactly,
it's more like a filmy, liquid cloud suspended in the air, a
water vacuole. You can see through it, but it's definitely dense
and impenetrable when it's closed.

A set of pincers emerges from inside the Tripod's head, passing
through the iris.

The pincers SNAP hard and grab hold of whatever's closest, and in
this case it's the ankle of one of the Teenagers, a boy about
seventeen.

He SCREAMS and the pincers retract. The Teenager is pulled hard,
sucked into the head of the Tripod, he's SCREAMING and he's up to
his knees, then his waist, then his shoulders, and hands are
reaching for him, trying to grab hold of him, but too late and too
weak.

He disappears into the head of the Tripod and the iris SLITHERS
shut again.

The basket abruptly levels itself, jarring everyone in it.

Fresh panic ensues. Whatever hands are closest SLAM against the
iris, but it's closed now, and impermeable. Inside, they can see
shadows moving, but that's it.

                              RAY (cont'd)
                    Rachel?! Take my hand!

He manages to make eye contact with Rachel and she fights to get
her hand to his, but there are too many people in the way.

But the Businesswoman can reach her and she manages to wrench her
own hand free. With it, she gets hold of Rachel's hand and pulls
her around, so that she can get hold of her father's hand.

They grab onto each other.

And the basket tilts again. Upright, at a forty-five degree
angle.

The six remaining humans SCREAM, they know what's next.

Ray looks up, sees the iris at the base of the basket start to
open. Ray's eyes pop wide, because the nearest human being this
time --

-- is Rachel.

Ray squirms himself around wildly, fighting to jockey himself
between Rachel and the opening iris. He violently pushes aside
other bodies and wriggles down near it, pushing Rachel off to the
side in the process. But he's ended up with his feet jammed right
against the iris.

The pincers emerge from inside the Tripod's head.

Ray looks down, and his right arm is trapped underneath somebody,
and that's the hand clutching the grenade belt.

Ray pulls hard, but can't get it free.

The pincers dart out and CLAMP DOWN HARD on Ray's feet, squeezing
them together and digging into his calves.

He grimaces as they dig into his flesh and he starts to move,
dragged down into the open iris.

                              RAY (cont'd)
                    THE BELT!!! THE BELT!

The Army Private, who is right next to him, turns and sees the
belt and understands in a minute what Ray intends to do. He
wriggles wildly, gets an arm free, uses it to lift the body
that's trapping Ray's right arm.

Ray's moving now, as the pincers retract the iris opens up into a sphincter-like opening that's pulling him in. He's up to his waist, half into the opening from which no one has ever returned.

Marshaling all his strength, he SNAPS his arm free and pulls it tight next to him, clutching the grenade belt.

> RACHEL
> (pawing at him)
> DADDY!!!

Ray is still moving, now he's in up to the middle of his chest. The Army Private and anyone else who is near enough grab hold of his shoulders or whatever else they can get their hands on, holding onto him with everything they've got, to prevent him from being sucked all the way inside.

One of Ray's hands is trapped in the sphincter, the one that's left free is still clutching the grenade belt, but Ray is SCREAMING in pain, the sphincter opening must be squeezing him like a boa constrictor, his whole face is turning red, his veins are bulging, he's in up to his neck now, one arm stretched out awkwardly (and unnaturally) in front of him.

Everybody in the basket is grabbing at him, trying like hell to keep him from going all the way in. But the sphincter-like device flexes tighter and tighter, and all at once, with a might sucking sound --

> RACHEL (cont'd)
> DADDY, NOOOO!!!

-- Ray is sucked all the way inside the head of the beast. Rachel SCREAMS in horror, but the Army Private refuses to give up, and before the sphincter completely closes he hurls himself at it, plunging both arms inside it.

The sphincter closes on his arms, but the Private has hold of something inside, and he twists himself around, gets both legs up against the edge of the thing --

> ARMY PRIVATE
> PULL ME!!!

-- and pulls hard, with everything he's got, everyone else in the basket pulling on him too.

All at once the sphincter CRACKS with a horrible wet CRUNCHING sound, it opens ever so slightly, and RAY BURSTS OUT, all at once, covered in a thick aqueous goo.

He lands in the middle of the group and rolls over, GASPING for air.

                                ARMY PRIVATE (cont'd)
                        The belt! Where's the grenade belt?!

Ray looks up at him and raises his right hand, which is balled up
into a fist. He opens it up, revealing a grenade pin in his palm.
It's at that moment --

-- *THE EXPLOSION COMES.*

It's two explosions, really, the first being one grenade going
off, and the other, a split-second later, much bigger as the rest
of the grenades on the belt explode as a result.

The shell of the Tripod's head explodes outward but does not
burst, absorbing most of the blast within its strong walls.

But the Tripod itself lurches, staggers like a punchy boxer.

(All of this is seen from inside the crazily bouncing basket.)

The basket rocks violently, the Tripod SLAMS into a tree on one
side, veers off, and its front leg telescopes halfway down all at
once, as if the thing is going to its knee.

Now rudderless, driverless, the Tripod's right rear leg attempts
two consecutive strides, and the whole thing pitches forward.

The ground races up at them fast and they SLAM into the earth,
dirt and mud flying everywhere, obscuring our vision and sending
up a thick cloud of debris.

146-159   OMITTED   146-159

160   WHEN THE DUST CLEARS,   160

all we see at first is a mass of mud. The mud starts to move,
arms and legs come out of it... somebody's head... *human beings,*
crawling out of the ooze, coming back to life.

We see Rachel's face first as she opens her eyes. She's no longer
in the basket, which has been wrenched free from the Tripod
wreckage by the violence of the fall.

The other bodies near her are moving too, everybody oozing out of
the mud into which they have fallen.

There's GASPING, CRYING. But they're alive. One of the bodies
rolls over near Rachel, and she finds herself face to face --

-- with her father. They crawl through the thick mud and grab
hold of each other.

                                                            CUT TO:

161   EXT   ABANDONED FREEWAY   DAY   161

A HORDE OF REFUGEES make their way down the middle of a highway,
strewn everywhere with dead cars.

A sign in the foreground tells us we're getting closer:

                        BOSTON   12

                                              CUT TO:

162   OMITTED   DAY   162

163   EXT   BOSTON - THE OLD CITY   DAY   163

A once-busy street in the heart of Boston. There's not a soul to
be seen, but destruction is everywhere -- rows and rows of empty
human clothing in the streets where bodies were vaporized, a
geyser of water spewing from a sheared fire hydrant no one was
there to cap, an overturned bus at the end of the street. The
front of a whole block of stores has been burned off. One, a
jewelry store, seems to have exploded into the street, leaving
expensive rings, watches, and necklaces strewn everywhere. But
no one has bothered to pick them up, they don't mean much
anymore.

The street stretches far into the distance, toward the river and
bridges far beyond, and it's the same empty, lonely story as far
as the eye can see. The most striking thing about the city is its
stillness.

And everywhere, the red weed, on buildings, on trees, everywhere.
There's something different about it here, something off, but we
don't have time to give it much thought, as Ray and Rachel come
around the corner and onto this abandoned block.

Ray looks down, at the water rushing through the street. The
gutters are swollen with red weed, huge rolling bundles of it all
along the water.

But Ray looks closer, because the red weed is dried out and
breaking. Great branches of it SNAP off and are swept into the
rushing stream, carried away by the same waters that initially
fed it.

That's weird. Ray turns to a patch of weed that has grown off a
tree on the sidewalk and SNAPS off a chunk of it. It's covered in
white spots, something like tonsillitis. He bends it. It's
brittle, and SNAPS in half at the slightest pressure.

Rachel leans over his shoulder and looks at the spots too.

163   CONTINUED: 163

                                    RACHEL
                         It looks sick.

                                     RAY
                         More than sick. It's dead. Or dying,
                         anyway.

              "ULLA!"

              Ray whirls, hearing the sound of a Tripod calling out in the
              distance, but it's bouncing off so many buildings they can't tell
              where it came from. Rachel instinctively grabs hold of him.

              The sound comes again, at regular intervals. They set off down
              the narrow streets of the city, in the opposite direction.

164   OMITTED   164

164A   EXT   BOSTON - INDUSTRIAL AREA   DAY   164A

              Ray and Rachel come around another corner and find a pack of
              birds, pecking at the pods that have grown from the red weed. But
              the pods are split open now, raw and fleshy and exposed, lying in
              the street.

              Ray and Rachel keep moving.

165   EXT   BOSTON - INDUSTRIAL AREA   DAY   165

              Ray and Rachel come around another corner and stop suddenly.

              The head of a Tripod is crashed in front of them.

              It's buried nose-first in the middle of the street. A hatch is
              partially open underneath its front, the lower lip of a slack-
              jawed mouth.

              Over and over, it BLEATS its recorded mechanical cry, and we
              realize why it sounded so plaintive -- it was calling for help.

              Ray and Rachel pass the frozen Tripod, waved along by a SOLDIER.

                                    SOLDIER 1
                         Keep moving. It's all right, you can
                         pass on through. Move along.

                                     RAY
                              (walking with Soldier)
                         What happened here?

                                    SOLDIER 1
                         Something's happening to them. Please
                         keep moving.

                              RAY
                Did you guys take it down?

                              SOLDIER 1
                No sir, it was behaving erratically.
                Walking in circles, and went down about
                an hour ago all by itself.

                              RACHEL
                Is it dead?

                              RAY
                Yes. Don't stop.

                              RACHEL
                How is it dead all by itself?

                              RAY
                Rachel, I don't know.

Suddenly, ANOTHER TRIPOD, perhaps coming to the aide of its
fallen comrade, emerges from the end of the street behind them
and walks forward. *Staggers* forward is more accurate, it's
barely able to stay on its feet. It SMASHES into the side of
another building, bouncing off and taking another unsteady step
forward.

VOICES rise up from around them, PEOPLE emerging from the mouths
of alleys, from buildings, from side streets -- a tentative
trickle at first, but there are more SOLDIERS, separated from
their units but still fighting.

The Tripod takes another step forward, shakily, about to go down.
THREE SOLDIERS take shelter on the alley wall opposite Ray and
Rachel.

As Ray watches, a BIRD circles around the head of the Tripod,
then lands on it. Ray furrows his brow, thinking. Now three more
birds land on top of the Tripod's head.

Ray thinks, there's something off about this, he's seen something
like it, he's trying to remember... and then his eyes light up.
He turns to the Soldiers and SHOUTS.

                              RAY (cont'd)
                Look at the birds!

But just as he speaks, the Tripod emits one of those piercing
cries of *"ULLA!"* and Ray's line is inaudible, we can only read
his lips.

                              SOLDIER
                What?!

>   RAY
>   (now audible again)
>   Look at the birds! Look at the God damn
>   birds!

The Soldiers all turn and look, but another *"ULLA"* blocks out
Ray's next line:

>   RAY (cont'd)
>   (blocked out by the *ULLA*)
>   No shield!

>   SOLDIER
>   What?!

Ray SHOUTS again, and this time his words burst through, and the
Soldier is able to hear and understand him:

>   RAY
>   *NO SHIELD!!!*

The Soldier, who carries a shoulder-borne missile launcher,
quickly realizes what this means and --

>   SOLDIER
>   *LOAD!*

-- another Soldier shoves a shell into the launcher. Ray whirls
and covers Rachel with his body as the shell ERUPTS out of the
tube and SLAMS into the side of the Tripod.

The resulting EXPLOSION is huge, and effective. The Tripod's
hull RIPS apart with a SHRIEK of torn metal. Rose-colored fluid
showers everywhere, the thing belches lifeblood, and the Tripod
pitches forward, first to one knee, and then careening all the
way down, SMASHING into the middle of the street.

Suddenly there's a commotion, and the crowd of people around the
first Tripod, the one with the hatchway hanging open, leaps back
as one, but crowds around it.

Ray moves forward. There's movement coming from inside the head
of the crashed Tripod, something slithering down that hatchway.

It's the forelimb of one of the invaders, moving weakly, near
death, trying to drag the bulky body down into the street.

But it has no strength left, it's covered in sickly white spots
like the red weed. Ray studies it, realizing something.

>   RACHEL
>   What happened? Did they get sick?

165   CONTINUED: (3)

                          RAY
               Yes they did.

                          RACHEL
               What from?

                          RAY
               Our germs. Maybe infection. Stuff
               we're immune to, that our bodies fight
               off every day.

The creeping forelimb stops, dead, still halfway in its ship.

                          RAY (cont'd)
               After everything we fought 'em with,
               they died from the air we breathe and
               the water we drink. All the things we
               need to live... that's what killed them.

PEOPLE advance slowly toward the hood of the Tripod, incredulous
and hopeful, and now more humans emerge from their hiding places,
crowding the streets.

                                                    CUT TO:

166   OMITTED   166

167   EXT   BOSTON - BROWNSTONE BLOCK   DAY   167

A neat row of townhouses in one of the oldest parts of Boston. We
settle on the front door of one particular house, we move in
toward it, and just as we reach it, the front door is yanked open
and *Mary Ann* is standing there, the kids' mom, alive and well.
She looks right at us and her face breaks with emotion, her hands
go involuntarily to her mouth, she rushes forward into the street
and finds Ray at the base of the stairs, carrying Rachel the last
few yards to her mother.

Ray smiles, deeply satisfied but feeling so keenly the loss of
Robbie. But then a pair of scuffed boots appear on the floor
behind Mary Ann and Rachel and Ray follows them up, disbelieving,
and of course the person standing there behind them is --

                          RACHEL
               ROBBIE!

It *is* Robbie, bruised and battered, but very much alive, standing
there in the doorway of his mother's house. He runs down the
stairs, kind of *falls* forward, into the street, into his father's
arms.

167 CONTINUED: 167

They hug each other, and Rachel hugs them both. Robbie finally
breaks down, the first time we've seen him crying, and in his
sobs we hear a word we haven't heard him say before:

                         ROBBIE
              ... Dad...

Robbie pulls away from his dad and goes to the doorway, drops to
his knees and holds his little sister and his mom. Ray watches,
incredulous, moved to tears, looking at his children.

Mary Ann looks up over the shoulders of Rachel and Robbie. Tears
stream from her eyes, she makes eye contact with Ray and mouths
two words -- "Thank you."

Tim appears in the hallway behind them, and their grandmother
too, hurrying down the stairs at the sound of the voices.

They all look at Ray, thanking him with their eyes, and beckoning
him inside. He walks up the steps, the door closes on all of
them, and an enormous CLANG --

168   EXT   BOSTON STREET   DAY   168

-- echoes as a BELL peals in the tower of a church steeple. The
heavy iron clapper SWISHES through frame and CLANGS again off the
side of the bell.

The VOICE OVER from the beginning returns as we start to rise up
the steeple of the church at the end of the block, shining gold in
the morning sun.

As we keep rising higher, it's only the second big, global view
of things we've seen in the movie -- this time, the morning sun
burns through the clouds over the skyline of Boston. In the
distance, the forms of Tripods are visible dotting the streets
everywhere. But none of them are moving. They're crashed, or
heeled over on their sides, stopped in their tracks.

We keep rising up and up, over the neighborhood, and we see four
or five church steeples in this old part of Boston, all with
their bells TOLLING jubilantly, calling SURVIVORS back into the
streets.

The branches of a tree come into frame, and as we move in among
the branches we zero in on a leaf, moving closer we see it's
covered with drops of water. The VOICE OVER from the beginning
comes back:

                         VOICE (O.S.)
              From the moment the invaders arrived,
              breathed our air, ate and drank, they
              were doomed.
                         (MORE)

                    VOICE (O.S.) (cont'd)
            They were undone, destroyed after all of
            humanity's weapons and devices had
            failed, by the tiniest creatures that
            God, in his wisdom, put upon this earth.

We keep moving, toward one drop in particular, and within that
drop we see the wriggling outlines of the tiny micro-organisms
that swarm and multiply within it.

                    VOICE (O.S.) (CONT'D)
            By the toll of a billion deaths, we have
            earned our immunity, our right to
            survive among this planet's infinite
            organisms --

As we go closer and closer and closer still, the drop fills the
frame, and we see the tens of thousands of squirming bacteria
inside that drop of water, and we think about how truly
significant they really are.

                    VOICE (O.S.) (CONT'D)
            -- and that right is ours against all
            challengers. For neither do we live nor
            die in vain.

                                  FADE OUT.

SCRIPT ADDENDUM

*S*ometimes on the day of shooting a lot of additional stray dialogue is required, especially for extras in crowd scenes. It's helpful to have that stuff written in advance, so the director doesn't have to think about it during a complex day or, worse, call you at home in a tizzy when you're in the middle of a sandwich.

Since dialogue of this type usually overlaps or plays completely in the background, including it in the shooting script can clog up the scene and obscure the real events, throwing off the reader's focus. So a few years ago I started putting stuff like this in appendix pages, where it's out of the flow of the script but still available to the director when he needs it.

In scene 13, a CNN NEWS ANCHOR is at the desk at CNN headquarters
in Atlanta. A map of the Ukraine is in a box on screen, and a
graphic in a banner across the bottom of the screen says "Deadly
Lightning Storm in Ukraine."

                         NEWS ANCHOR
              The Ukraine, a country of some fifty-two
              million people, is in almost total
              blackness tonight in the wake of a
              series of freakish lightning storms of
              catastrophic proportions which struck
              the country at approximately 4 a.m.
              local time. The Associated Press is
              estimating two hundred dead in the
              sweeping blackouts which have paralyzed
              the country and cut off nearly all
              communication with the outside world.

In the middle of the above report, the Bartender picks up the
remote and switches the TV over to ESPN, where a SPORTS ANCHOR is
reporting over footage of a BASEBALL PLAYER.

                        SPORTS ANCHOR
              As usual, George Steinbrenner wasted no
              time getting out his checkbook this off-
              season, signing free agent right fielder
              Marcus Williams to a reported three
              year, fifty-eight million dollar
              contract yesterday in Milwaukee.
              Williams, who is thirty-eight, batted
              .262 with the Brewers last year,
              pounding out 31 home runs and 85 RBIs.

CONTINUED:

APPENDIX AA

Suggested dialogue for BYSTANDERS at the five-corner intersection, before the ground starts to rumble:

> LOCAL GUY
> Never seen anything like it! It was like a, like a, lightning squall or something.

> LOCAL WOMAN
> I was standing right over there, I'd just come out of the store, and it struck right in front of me, I couldn't have been more than twenty feet away from it.

> LOCAL WOMAN 2
> You're lucky you're alive! You could have been killed!

> LOCAL WOMAN
> Over and over and over, it just kept striking and striking and striking.

> UNIFORMED COP
> You could *smell* it, is the weird thing, this smell in the air, just hanging there, like burnt toast or something.

> FIREMAN
> This whole block should be on fire, is the amazing thing, nothing caught, I've never seen anything like it.

> CONCERNED MOTHER
> I went over to the school, there were a few other parents there, but they sent us away, I don't know, do you think we should get the kids? Maybe we should pick up the kids.

> MAN WITH KID
> Don't get too close! Kevin, I said not too close, c'mon, get away from there.

> HIGH SCHOOL KID
> Check this! You gotta see this, get up here, look at this!

> ### FRAZZLED MAN
> -and then the car went dead, just like
> that, but it kept rolling I couldn't
> stop, I was rolling right straight
> toward it, it just kept flashing in
> front of me, over and over and over, I
> thought I was going to roll straight
> into it!

> ### WIDE-EYED WOMAN
> I was completely blinded! Couldn't see
> a thing, my eyes were burning, I thought
> I'd been hit, I did, I thought I'd been
> struck by lightning!

And then, as the RUMBLING begins and the ground starts shaking:

> ### JULIO
> Hey, you feel that? What is that, the
> subway?

> ### RAY
> Subway doesn't run under here.

> ### JULIO
> PATH train, maybe?

> ### RAY
> Not this far west.

APPENDIX B

Some suggested dialogue for a few members of the Crowd in Scene 30, when the windows start to crack:

                    DELI OWNER
          The windows are breaking, get away from
          the windows!

                    POLICEMAN
          Lady, get the hell away from there,
          watch out for the glass!

                    BEAUTY SALON LADY
          It's an earthquake! Get into a doorway,
          it's the only safe place!

                    POLICEMAN
          What the hell is the matter with you,
          the glass is breaking all over the God
          damn place, I said get away from there!

                    DOG OWNER
          Arbus?! Arbus, get back here! ARBUS!

                    PANICKY WOMAN
          Oh my God, what is happening, God no, no
          no, no please, what in the name of Jesus
          is happening?!

                    DELI WORKER
          Get some plywood, as quick as you can!
          Board up everything before it explodes!

                    SECOND POLICEMAN
          I got no radio! Dead air on everything!
          Send Lopez back to the station, we need
          a dozen patrol cars out here RIGHT NOW!

                    POLICEMAN
          Clear the area! People! People,
          please, we need you to clear the area
          RIGHT NOW!

                    CONCERNED MOTHER
          Ernesto! Get your brother and pull him
          away from there, get him out of there,
          GET HIM OUT OF THERE!

APPENDIX C

Some suggested dialogue for the crowd in Scene 77, when Ray is confronting the people who are stealing the car, while Rachel is still in it.

> REASONABLE WOMAN
> Stop it, stop it, both of you for God's sake, stop what you're doing!

> AGGRESSIVE GUY
> Get the gun! Somebody get the gun! Grab him!

> CONSERVATIVE GUY
> Get away from the gun! Don't touch him, move away from the guns!

> UNARMED POLICEMAN
> Put 'em down, both of you, before somebody gets killed here!

> CONSPIRACY GUY
> This doesn't have to happen like this! Listen to me, please, both of you, just lower the guns and we can work this out!

> JUDGMENTAL GUY
> You're crazy, you're both crazy, you're killing each other, that's exactly what they want!

> NEARBY PARENT
> Get away from them, Tommy, get behind me! Move, move, MOVE!

> LAW & ORDER GUY
> Where's a cop?! Somebody call a cop!

APPENDIX D

Suggested dialogue for Ray in Scene 106, when he and Robbie are struggling on the ground near the hilltop and Ray is shouting into Robbie's ear:

> RAY
>
> Don't do it, I am begging you, I'm telling you, do not do this. I know you want to fight, I know it seems like you have to, but you don't, this is your *life*, the only life you get, and it's gonna be *over*, you will *die*, do you understand me, if you go over that hilltop you are going to be killed. I'm not gonna let you, you can hate me as much as you want, but I love you and I'm not gonna let you do it, Robbie, I love you, listen to me, I know what I'm saying! Don't go! Don't go! DO NOT GO!

Q & A

WITH DAVID KOEPP
BY ROB FELD

O n June 23, 2005, the morning before *War of the Worlds* premiered in New York City, Rob Feld sat down with David Koepp in his office to discuss the new film and his work.

Let's start out with your background: where you were born, where you came from.

David Koepp: Pewaukee, which is a little town of about 3,000 people in southern Wisconsin. I started out wanting to be an actor and went to the University of Wisconsin, Madison, for two years for acting. But, while I was a very good actor in Pewaukee—in fact one of the twenty or thirty best—when I got to a really big city like Madison, I found that I was not. But I was also writing, and it just hadn't occurred to me that you could write movies until I saw *Raiders of the Lost Ark* in 1981. For some reason, in that movie I sensed the writer, you know? I don't know why. You know the scene where you think there's going to be a big bullwhip and scimitar fight, and then Indy just shoots the guy? It occurred to me that somebody had to think of that. Somebody had to say, "We'll make 'em think it's going to be this, but it'll actually be that."

What were you writing?

DK: Plays, and they all had about thirty-seven scenes in them, so my playwriting professor said, "You might want to think about movies." So I went to UCLA film school and just kept writing scripts.

So how did you get your first script, **Apartment Zero,** *made?*

DK: I got an internship with a sales agent who worked for foreign distributors. We'd buy B and C titles from the United States for video distribution in their country, like *Sorority House Massacre III*, and stuff like that. I was working for him as an intern/assistant, writing scripts at night and when he was out of town. He introduced me to Martin Donovan (not the actor) and we wrote *Apartment Zero* together. It was an indie suspense psychosexual bit of weirdness. I think it reflects Martin's personality more than it does mine, but I'm really proud of it. I think I had a sense of structure and he had a great sense of character and story, and visual sensibility. Then we wrote *Death Becomes Her* together, which is another lurid piece of cool weirdness. And that was it. *Apartment Zero* cost $1.2 million, but we only raised about $800,000 going in. By that point I was employable because I had written *Bad Influence*, so I took any rewrite I could get to pay off the mix and the storage fees until we found a distributor.

Did you find that writing genre was a good start? Many people, from Peter Jackson to Bill Condon, got their starts that way.

DK: Yeah, absolutely. I still write genre, I love it. *War of the Worlds* is very much a genre movie—it's a horror movie. I think people disdain genre or look down their nose at it at their own peril. Once in a while some horror or suspense movie comes along that's kind of high-toned, and you know it's in trouble when, in the interviews, the director starts saying, "We wanted to elevate the genre." Fuck you, elevate the genre! The genre's perfectly fine. It doesn't need your elevation. Those movies usually turn out to be turgid pieces of crap. You have to respect and enjoy genre. *Double Indemnity*'s a genre film—you think that was easy? So I love it, and when you ask most people what their favorite movies are, they're going to be genre films. *The Godfather*'s a genre movie; it's a gangster movie. It's not exactly the old Warner Bros. model, but it's a gangster movie.

So what is a genre film? Why are archetypical stories so powerful?

DK: It's a movie where you know very much what it is, like it wouldn't be hard to determine what shelf it belongs on in the video store. There are rules and expectations of each genre, which is nice because you can go in and consciously meet them, or upend them, and we like it either way.

Upend our expectations and we love it—though it's harder—or meet them and we're cool with it because that's all we really wanted that night at the movies anyway. The more challenging movies are ones that defy description or categorization, and those are the real trick. Those are like writing a hit pop song or hitting a curve ball; they're narrowly focused, difficult things to do.

Tell me a bit about your philosophy of writing a script. What goes on a page and what doesn't? I've read the scripts for both **War of the Worlds** *and* **Secret Window**, *and they're both very literary or prosaic, when the classic Syd Field instruction, for what it's worth, is to simply put what you see on screen and avoid comment. But you have a voice, sometimes speaking directly to the reader.*

In **Secret Window**, *for example, you wrote, "He gets out, leaving the door hanging open, the car* BINGING *at him about the keys, the lights, you're doing everything wrong." It's very effective and evocative. So tell me what you see as your job, as you're putting words on the page.*

DK: I think you have to do that sort of thing—and you have to do it without getting obnoxious and slowing the movie down—but anywhere you can slip in personality, feeling or vibe is going to help the read. I think the screenwriter's first job is to evoke the movie on paper, and that's really hard. I know a lot of people who have very good movies in their heads, but cannot put them on paper. Those people are called *directors*. I always saw the screenwriter's job as getting the conversation started, because nobody can start talking about a movie until they know what kind of movie it's supposed to be.

You're trying to take something that's all about sound and visuals and type it, and that's really hard. So anytime I can find some turn of phrase or some technique to manipulate words on paper into the feeling of a movie, I'll grab it.

I remember two things that taught me a lot. I read Kubrick's script for *2001: A Space Odyssey* a long time ago, and I got to a point where there were a couple of blank pages. I thought it was some Xeroxing error, but after three or four of them, I got to a point that just said, in the middle of the page, "The spaceship docks." And then there were three more blank pages after it. I got it. It was the big scene and he didn't feel like typing the whole thing. Having already seen the movie, I felt it completely captured that first scene where the spaceship docks; the feeling of air and time and slowness that it had. I think you have to look for opportunities like that.

The other thing that taught me a lot was during *Death Becomes Her*. There's a moment where Meryl Streep's character is at the top of a staircase teetering, and her husband decides to push her down the stairs—he just reaches out and pushes her with one finger. But I wrote, "She hangs there at the top of the stairs, defying the laws of physics like Wile E. Coyote for a moment, until PLING, he pushes her and she falls." Bob Zemeckis said that line of description was what made him want to do the movie, because he felt, "I get it, it's exaggerated, it's like a cartoon." So, if you can find those....

Useful also, I imagine, because you have to communicate tone and voice, as well as what one sees.

DK: Yes, but there's a real danger of falling in love with your own witticisms. Then you become obnoxious and you've got to know where to stop.

Are you also thinking while writing that ultimately there's going to be a director interpreting this, and while you want to tell him as much of what this is as possible, you don't want to strap him down or—

DK: It's not strapping him down because, God knows, they will not allow that, but you have to trick them a little bit. If you refer specifically to the camera, or some sort of shot or approach, it's pretty much a guarantee that it won't be in the movie. Even if they think it's brilliant, they're just not going to use it because they will not be told by some fucking *writer* how to shoot their movie.

Yet in the opening of **War of the Worlds** *you have a line describing, "One of those long-lens shots looking down Sixth Avenue in Manhattan as the workday lets out." Did that come out of discussion, or did you just put that in there?*

DK: I put it in there and Steven shot it, which surprised me. But writing for Spielberg is a little different because he's never threatened. Also, if you say, "It's one of those long-lens shots down Sixth Avenue," you know exactly what you're driving at—that one from *Tootsie*, when he's walking toward the camera in drag for the first time. Everybody knows what that shot is, so I felt like that was okay. But yeah, I did sort of break my own rule there.

Is it different to write for a director you know well? Do you write in his voice?

DK: You may do it without even trying. The directors I've written for the most are Steven and Brian De Palma, and they both have such distinctive methods of expression. As moviegoers, we know their voices really intimately. It's very hard not to have that voice in your head when you're writing, and you might as well because you should write what you think that director will do well.

You can write stuff that you know they're not going to like, or you know isn't quite up their alley, but if they chafe at it, you're better off cutting it. I've tried the thing of forcing directors to do something, and what happens is you either get fired or they'll say, "Sure, sure, sure," and then not do it. Or they'll do it, because they have good intentions, and it won't come out well because they didn't see it, they didn't mean it, and they didn't feel it. It has to be theirs, and you might as well not even fight against that.

Good directors don't record your screenplay, they interpret it, which means changing it and making it their own. And if they don't, then they're hacks. That's why I don't like to be on set during production unless there's a specific issue to address. You know, you go and you're bored because there's nothing for you to do, and apparently I have a tendency to sit in a chair and wince, which is probably not encouraging to everybody. And you can't sit there like the word police. They've got to do their thing. It's better for them if you're not there because they're less inhibited, and it's better for you if you're not there because you don't want to see that sausage made. Go home and plan the movie you're going to direct yourself, and let them do their thing.

One thing you do on the page is set location very well and specifically. There's that cheap, drywall motel you describe in Secret Window, "a twelve-cabins-twelve-vacancies kind of place," and you get it, you know that

motel. Can you talk about location as character, and not just skipping to the action?

DK: Well, of course "twelve-cabins-twelve-vacancies" is lifted from some Norman Bates dialogue in *Psycho*, so it always helps to steal from good sources. I think that you abdicate your responsibility if you don't pick *where*. Part of your job is to ask, where does this take place? Who are they? It's not Anytown, USA. You can't recognize Anytown, USA, that's not a specific. You'd also be giving up your one shot at input. They're probably going to disregard where you picked to shoot, but you might as well give it a shot. On *War of the Worlds*, I was enamored of this neighborhood in Newark, called the Ironbound, that I felt was really photogenic and unusual. You don't see that kind of rust-belt, working-class neighborhood in American films too much, at least not in big studio movies. It's always the suburbs or Fifth Avenue or just dirt poor. It's as if there are no other places to shoot. But the vast majority of people live in that kind of middle-class housing. So I wrote it for the Ironbound and was surprised that they liked it. I assumed we were going to get moved to San Diego or something. Perhaps, in part, because they needed pre-production to go quickly, they showed up and were very happy with it. But that's unusual. You almost always end up having to change or move it, or face reality in one way or another.

Perhaps this is an obvious point about writing, but your vocabulary is extensive and precise. In scene 30 of War of the Worlds, *you wrote, "A beveled pad rises out of the bottom and claws into the earth, stabilizing itself. Then, as one, the three legs WHIR to life and exert pressure inward." It's dense yet concise, and gives a tactile sense of the movement of the tripod. Before you start a certain kind of script, do you go looking for words for the mechanics of what you're going to have to describe?*

DK: Well, certainly if you do any research, it pops up in your writing, but the danger in that is how much is too much, how far do you go? You can never stop the reader's eye, or slow it down, or give them a reason to go to the bathroom. That's the real trick in writing screenplays. Screenplays are awful to read—there's really nothing worse than being asked to read a screenplay. It's the worst thing that can happen to you as a reader because they're just bad reading experiences. There's all that white space and the inexplicable capital letters—I still don't understand when I'm supposed to capitalize and when I'm not. I don't get it. I do try to break up the description with a lot of white space, and the double dashes where one thing leads to another, so you can just keep the eye moving. But, in terms of vocabulary, I'm just trying to find an economical and precise way to say it.

Everybody still assumes that all the screenwriter does is write dialogue and characters, and they figure that when you come to an action sequence, you just bleep past it and wait for the director to fill it in. That's just so offensive. More than half our job is figuring out how to tell a story with pictures. We design the action scenes first. They redesign them, surely, but sometimes they don't. Sometimes they just shoot what you wrote. So describing action and finding the right words to describe it is a huge part of what we do, but making it clear is essential. People have to be able to read a script and see a good movie, and if they can't see it, they won't make it.

Let's venture into* War of the Worlds *now. Tell me how the project came to you and what your initial conversations with Spielberg were about?

DK: Steven called and asked if I wanted to do *War of the Worlds*. I said, "I don't know, I haven't thought about it for a while. Let me read it and refresh my memory." Before I did, though, my first thought was not so much concern that the book had been done before—it was a radio show, a movie, and there was a rock-and-roll musical version in the 70s—but that it falls into two genres that are really well-trod—alien invasion and disaster movie. I wondered what ground had been left uncovered that we could possibly stake out as our own?

After I reread it, though, I was amazed to find that the best idea in the book was the one no one had ever used: this idea of showing a vast global event from a very limited perspective, only through the eyes of this unnamed narrator.

Now, I named him, because I'm not as brave as H. G., but I thought that if we can make a rule that we will not see anything unless Ray [played by Tom Cruise] sees it, and we'll not know anything unless Ray knows it, then we have an interesting way into the movie, and it could become a much more personal, intimate and powerful movie than it would be if we went so broad scope as to show the Taj Mahal and the Great Wall of China and the President of the United States and the Chairman of the Joint Chiefs, and a bunch of people on TV screaming at each other. If we made a list of all those clichés and forbade ourselves from doing any of them, then it would be like the Hays Code; the constraint would force us to think of other ways of solving problems and imparting information.

Exposition, in particular, was a real bitch in this, because all we could know was what information came to Ray, or what he could figure out by himself. But, since he's a dockworker and not a scientist, what he's able to figure out isn't much. So I thought, well, if *that's* the approach, I think I can do that.

Then the writing of the first draft followed standard first draft pace, because Steven was going to do his Munich Olympics movie and there seemed to be no real rush. I think I did three or four months of thinking and outlining, and then wrote the first draft in about eight weeks, so a total of about six months for a first draft, which is more or less normal when you're not in a hurry.

The first draft went over really well, so then the rush to production started. I was thrilled that they wanted to start shooting quickly because that just meant less development—I don't care how good anybody is, development pretty much kills you because you just keep going at stuff that might work because you're bored with it after three years.

It's impossible for me to start a discussion about the development of the story without entering through the 9/11 prism. Was there much discussion with Spielberg about the story and its references to 9/11; about what this was going to be about?

DK: Well, two answers; first about the story in general. Steven generally has a bunch of ideas up front, but then he'll stop talking and say, "Now I want to see what you think." He knows perfectly well he'll have influence over the script in any way he chooses, so he doesn't want to bigfoot the writer before he even starts. I think he figures he paid for your opinion, and he wants to see it—then he'll tell you if you're wrong.

So, after the first draft, if you've got his attention and he's interested, your phone never stops ringing because he's got 150 ideas and they just keep coming. A bad sign with Steven is when you turn in a draft and he only has two or three comments, because that means his imagination didn't get engaged and the project is probably going to die.

As for 9/11, certainly this story has vast political implications. In the late 1890s, it was about British imperialism; in the late 1930s, it was about the fear of Fascism; in the early 1950s, it was the Commies are coming to get us; and now it can be read two ways—it could be post-9/11 American fear of terrorism, which is certainly there in the movie, but I bet if you see this movie in France, it will be about Iraq and fear of an American invasion. What's interesting about the story is that every time it's transplanted to a new time and place, it immediately becomes about the local or world politics.

So we felt better to not say or do anything in particular, because it would happen anyway. If we got the story and characters right, then the themes would rise out of it.

As for specific 9/11 references—like Dakota's character saying, "Is it the terrorists?" or when Tom is covered in ash—those weren't put in because of 9/11; they were put in because we all lived through 9/11. We all come out of the same set of experiences, and we just decided not to censor ourselves, because that's not realistic, that's not the world we live in.

In the first draft Dakota didn't have that line, but Steven said, "Wouldn't she think it's terrorists?"

And I said, "Well, yeah, but do we really want to evoke that, do we want to come out and say it?"

And he said, "But she would, she's 11."

And it's true, she would. So she did.

Don't you think the most resonant films become about more than what they're about? Is action just about action? Frequently not, it's usually a metaphor for something.

DK: But in the best films metaphors and themes surface on their own. Anybody who leads with their themes or politics is really, really going to make a bad movie. But if you just keep saying to yourself, "No, no, no, no, no—it's just a little survival story about this little family," then it has a chance of taking on some universality or larger meaning. There's an old expression about writing: if you aim for the general, you're going to miss everything, but if you aim for the specific, you have a shot at the universal. So I kept thinking, the smaller I make the family drama at the center, the better it's going to be. It just got smaller and smaller and smaller—limit the characters as much as humanly possible, just make the drama between these three people. So that's what I tried to do.

Limited information can be a terrifying and suspense-creating tool, especially in a total information age like ours. You used it in a similar way in **Trigger Effect,** *during the blackout. One of the awful things on 9/11 was that we had no idea what was going on.*

DK: Yeah. My most vivid memory of 9/11, thankfully, is fairly benign. I was standing on Central Park West in front of my kids' school. I had gone to pick them up as soon as I heard that something bad was happening downtown, but the school wanted to dismiss everybody at the same time. So we all had to stand there until noon, because a lot of the parents worked in the Trade Center and they didn't want rumors spreading and children terrified. From 9:30 'til noon, I was standing on the front steps with all these other parents, and nobody had any information because cell phones weren't working. So everything passed by word of mouth, and sometimes it would be wrong. First I heard both towers had fallen, then I heard no, it's only one.

That was really scary to me, that we couldn't get our hands on the truth. I think that's what scares us the most, obviously, is not knowing. And that's why Orson Welles' radio show worked so well. What's great is you get about five minutes of dance music up front, and then you get maybe forty-five seconds of information, and then another five minutes of dance music. People must have been clawing at their radio speakers to get words out of it!

So, I thought the first thing we had to come up with was a device to remove all modern conveniences. Telephones, televisions, radios—everything has to be out of commission, so that the only information you can get is from other human beings. And once we did that, then it became really frightening and upsetting because you don't know what's going on.

If something happens, the first thing we do is turn on the television, and if we see that *Days of Our Lives* is still on, then we know it wasn't so bad. We understand CNN and MSNBC are going to start running full time coverage, but when the networks kick in, that's when you know you'd better stop and watch. If you don't have that gauge, it's scarier. Of course, if you see a tripod with a heat ray walking down the street, you're pretty sure it's a significant event, but that removal of information was key to telling the whole story.

Radio drama, though, blows film out of the water. It's capable of so much more because it enlists the listener, who has to provide half the information. It's a cliché, but human imagination is much better than any screenwriter or director.

Did you talk about the look and functioning of the tripods before starting work? Did you have any conversations with effects guys, or did you start with a blank page?

DK: Well, I had pretty vivid descriptions from the book—of course, 107 years old—but I asked Steven, "I'm about to write the first tripod scene, do you have any sketches or thoughts?" And he said, "I have thoughts, but I don't want to tell you until after you write it," which is, of course, the maddening response. So you just make up whatever you see in your head and describe it, like that one sentence you mentioned, with as much detail as possible without being ponderous. Then, once you see the sketches, you go back and revise a little bit to make sure that you don't have some wildly contradictory description in there.

So let's talk, then, about how you took what was in the 107-year-old book, and how you adapted it to what would work now, for this story in this day and age. The script opens with a view of an inhospitable planet, which didn't make it into the film. But, obviously, you wanted to use that to frame motivation for these aliens.

DK: That's what I wanted to do, and I felt that a couple shots intercutting the lushness of our planet with the barren surface of theirs would answer that right up front, and we'd never have to worry about it again. Steven felt that, since we never go to another planet in the movie, it seemed out of character. Why can't we just stay on earth? He also felt it was self-evident what the aliens wanted—they clearly want our planet and they have a problem with *us*. He felt, "What else do you have to know? *Run!* is what you have to know," which I think is bold and works. The movie, as we speak, hasn't opened yet, so we'll see what most people think of that.

And the thought of having the tripods underground, amidst us like sleeper cells—

DK: That was an idea Steven had before I even came to the project. He just felt that we've seen aliens hurtling through space and landing on our planet, so let's try something different. In the book, they see the flashes on Mars and shuttles fly through space and land here. But, because we're in a technologically sophisticated world now, we would see this stuff coming weeks away. We'd know something's coming and there'd be endless analysis on TV, by pipe-smoking scientists, of what it was and why—and we really wanted to avoid all that.

So the idea of them bursting up from underground, where they've been for a thousand years, seemed a fresh way to approach it. I always figured we were the aliens' contingency plan. A thousand years ago they saw that their planet was going south, and they said, "We're going to try to fix it. If we can't fix it, let's just plant some stuff on this other planet in case we ever need to move."

You must have had concerns about the **deus ex machina** *ending, where the aliens die because of what was here already, with no direct human intervention in their destruction. How did you start thinking about and pre-empting that, so we wouldn't feel that at the end?*

DK: Well, the book is more of an experience than a story, so I think some of us will still feel it. But I made the first shot of the movie a shot of microbes, and my assumption is that this story is so well known, maybe two thirds of the audience going in knows that bacteria killed them in the book. And the first shot of the movie says, "You remember how bacteria killed them in the book? Well, it's going to kill them in the movie, too."

It is a *deus ex machina*, literally—we even say at the end, "God in his wisdom put them here"—but that's okay with me, because the *plot* of the movie is aliens come, they fight for a while, and they're killed by bacteria. But the *story* of the movie is about a father who won't do anything for his kids, goes on this journey, protects them for a long time, and at the end, turns into a father who will do anything for his kids, including kill or die.

That's the story, that's what I was interested in, that's the one that needed a beginning, middle and end.

As for aliens coming and how they're defeated, that's just not a movie that I think is that interesting anymore. We could have had a sequence where Tom reveals his hidden skills as a fighter jet pilot and figures out how to get into the mother ship, but that just wasn't a movie we were interested in.

So I saw no reason not to use an ending that's worked for 107 years. The problem is, it's an anticlimax, so you're building a whole movie to an anticlimax. But then I thought, "Fuck it, that might be kind of fun. Why not give that a try? I'm tired of climaxes." Some people might chafe, but that's okay. They'll survive.

And Ray still knocks off an alien or two.

DK: He knocks off one, the Army knocks off another one, and God takes care of the rest. We also set it up in subtler ways. Early on Dakota's character has a splinter and she says, "My body will just push it out," which was us saying, "This is a metaphor, get ready, it's going to be germs again."

So, hopefully that worked. I think it worked. I liked it. In the book, Welles had a narrator and a God's-eye view. He was able to finish off the aliens and say, "Look, it was bacteria," and then take his narrator home, where he is happily reunited with his wife, which is the last moment in the movie.

I wanted to do it that way—have it revealed that it's bacteria, then have the family reunion as the last image in the movie, but we absolutely couldn't because we wanted it all to take place in this compressed time period. We had a draft where Tom's character figured out that it must have been bacteria that killed the aliens before the family is reunited—and it just seemed ludicrous. Why on earth would this guy be able to get to the bottom of things that way?

So what stays and what goes as you adapt a book? Is it thematic even more than anything? Put the original aside and see what you can do with it?

DK: Adaptations are so much easier than an original script, of course, because you have the benefit of someone else thinking for a couple years. I go back and scene-card the entire book, look at that outline, and then despair for a while that it's so un-filmlike. Then I start throwing out stuff that I've always hated, or didn't think would work in the movie, but hold on to everything that I think is cool, finding any way I possibly can to keep it, and see what interstitial material I need to write to unite it all. Then, as the drafts develop, it increasingly becomes its own story and less episodic. But you try to hold on to the stuff that made you love the book.

In the outline I had a long sequence with the black smoke from the book, for a while, that never quite made it into the script. It was this great scene where, after they wipe out everything with the heat ray, the tripods would come through and disperse this black smoke that would kill everybody who breathed it. It was great because it had a life—it crept and rolled and climbed. In the scene, Ray and the kids found they were in this great open field when the black smoke starts rolling in, and there's no high ground—you have to get about ten feet off the ground to avoid it. There are trees in the distance so they run and climb them, but they're very young trees, so they start to bend over. It was kind of cool, but there was so much action in that segment of the movie, in the end we didn't have room for it.

How do you think about constructing an action scene like that, where characters are okay, they're not; they're okay, they're not; they're up a tree, it bends....

DK: I think those moments are what make storytelling exciting. There's a kids' book, actually, called *That's Good! That's Bad!* that I always thought perfectly encapsulates storytelling. It's about a kid who falls off a mountain, and somebody says, "That's bad," but somebody else says, "No, that's good, because then he caught the legs of a migrating stork." "Oh," they say, "that's good." "No, that's bad, because the stork flew into a storm," and it goes on.

It's timeless and cross-cultural. There's a classic Chinese tale just like that, where a farmer's horse runs away, which is bad, but then returns bringing more wild horses, which is good, but then his son breaks his leg riding one, which is bad, but then can't go to war, which is good, on and on and on.

DK: Well, reversals are what make storytelling interesting. I think it's great that in the cellar, after Ray goes through everything he does, and ends up deciding to kill a man in cold blood to protect them from the probe, you cut, and the very next scene, the probe's staring right at his daughter. Whether he killed the man or not, it would have been there anyway.

Something I've noticed you do—and I think many good writers do—is implanting echoes, if that's what I can call them. For example, the body rejects Dakota's splinter as the earth will reject the aliens; or seeing Ray as a crane operator, which looks an awful lot like the aliens manipulating the tripods. Tell me about how that functions in the script, what that does, how that helps, how you start thinking about these things?

DK: Some of it you do for yourself, and some of it happens by accident. I wish I could say I made him a crane operator because I thought it would look like the tripods, but really I just wanted him to be a dockworker. I don't know why, it just sort of popped into my head. Then I went online and saw what those big container cranes look like, so that was just a bonus.

The splinter was a conscious attempt to set something up, not in a story way, but in a thematic way. E. M. Forster wrote, "Only connect." Writing is all about connecting, and any time you connect one thing to another, it makes your story better. The more connections you have, the better your story is. So I'm always on the lookout for those. Sometimes they just happen while you're writing and sometimes they happen without your knowledge, and you take credit for them later.

*Tell me about one of the films you wrote and directed, **Trigger Effect**, and what you took from that experience. It was also about people escaping in a power outage, with no supplies and no information. Obviously, by* **War of the Worlds**, *you had thought a great deal about what that experience is.*

DK: I think that *Trigger Effect* was really a response to the birth of my first son—you're very melodramatic when your first child is born. You tend to think in apocalyptic scenarios. The first time you hold him, you think, I must protect this child, what would I do to protect this child, to what lengths would I go? The truth is we're not cavemen, we don't really have to go to such great lengths, but you do feel stirrings of those very primitive feelings of protection and responsibility.

Also, the idea of throwing the modern world back into a more primitive time is appealing in part because it's dangerous, and we start to think about what that would be like, if we weren't so buttoned down all the time. It's also sexy, because for some reason we think that would mean we would get to fuck a lot. I don't know why. *[Laughs]* It's because the lights go out.

There's a great line in *Body Heat* when somebody says, "When the temperature goes up people go crazy, people think the ordinary rules don't apply." Which we somehow do. When some element of civilization, some veneer, is removed, we think we can act in a different way.

So that stuff had been on my mind, and that sort of disaster planning. *Trigger Effect*, though, is essentially about a bunch of suburban people over-reacting, whereas in *War of the Worlds*, everyone's reacting properly to a really scary scenario.

It is something you write about frequently, though—that veneer and the darkness beneath, like Lord of the Flies. *As long as everything's pretty much copasetic, we're okay. But as soon as we get scared, or threatened, or something's being taken from us—*

DK: Yeah—we get ugly.

We get ugly.

DK: Well, it's interesting. We were in a story meeting one day, when I was maybe halfway through the *War of the Worlds* script. I had shown the first half to Steven and he said, "I want you to remember, though, that in times of great disaster and crisis like this, it does tend to bring out the best in people, and you've got to look for those moments where you can find the goodness of man." I said, "Yes, you're absolutely right," and went home and wrote the carjacking scene, where it's as ugly as ugly gets. In part, because I'm still a teenager and I have to rebel against Dad, but also because I thought, "Steven, because you're a very hopeful and optimistic man, I'm just going to trust you to find those moments of goodness, and I'll take responsibility for the darkness because that's more in line with my world-view." He is genuinely hopeful and optimistic, and I'm not. And so my hope was that if I handle the shadows, he'll handle the light and we'd balance out somewhere in between.

I've also seen you use extended moments of black screen a few times. In scene 56 of the War of the Worlds *script, you wrote, "We're going for a record for on-screen blackness here," and in* **Stir of Echoes** *you also have an extended period of black screen—*

DK: I just figure that my resources are so limited, I've got to pull in any tool I can. I like it in *War of the Worlds*. I wish Steven had held it even longer. But, you know, maybe black screen isn't the most popular thing. People might figure that's not what they paid their 10 bucks for.

Isn't it in **Wait Until Dark** *where—*

DK: Yeah—it's only lit by the light of the refrigerator. I saw that when I was a freshman in high school. I saw Waukesha North High School's production of *Wait Until Dark*, and the refrigerator scene scared the living shit out of me. These were high school actors—I can't imagine it was really all that good, but I just found it terrifying.

I guess, since it's your propensity to go darker, the scripts you write to direct yourself tend to be more psychological thriller than action. Tell me what consistently interests you, the questions that you find yourself starting with.

DK: Well, it's changing a little. The next thing I want to direct is a comedy that I'm writing now with John Kamps. You get tired of the same-old, same-old. I remember when I was writing *Panic Room*. I had just started and Brian De Palma asked what I was working on. I told him, and that I was worried that it's more of the same old thing—upper-middle-class people, frightened and trapped—and he said, "Hey, it's called who you are." That was true, but maybe now I don't feel quite as frightened and trapped as I did a few years ago. So I'm trying different things. But you never know what attracts you or why, and I think it's best not to question it too much, because you could disappear right up your own ass.

Let's get back to looking at what happens when that veneer gets stripped away—we scratch below that surface of the social compact and all too suddenly we find fewer reasons to be so polite to one another. I don't know if it's animal—

DK: Sure it is, I mean it's totally animal. I think *War of the Worlds* is a survival story, about how far will you go to survive? How far will you go to protect your children? But it's also a survival story for the aliens, which is what's interesting. And they're not really villains. I remember on *Jurassic*

Park, we were never allowed to refer to them as *monsters*—we were supposed to call them *animals*. And the aliens in this movie are animals, too. You could tell the same story again from the point of view of the aliens, and it would be a tragedy. Their planet is dying—they're just looking for a place where they can survive.

Taking that perspective, there's the comparison in the book of aliens are to men as men are to ants—and in the film it's men and maggots, right?

DK: Yes, you know, the aliens probably had a lengthy debate on their planet about whether we had consciousness or not. And they decided, well, if they were so smart would they be using spray-on deodorant? The way they devised to eliminate us was very humane. I mean, the heat ray is not painful—you're running in terror one second and you're vaporized the next, so I don't think they're so bad. In the movie, when they come down into that basement, they seem curious and interested, they seem frightened.

I think it's important to remember everybody's motivation is ultimately animal, because it is. Everything we do has an animal basis. We hold hands with our loved one because it's a tie sign, not because we so enjoy clutching each other, but to tell everyone in the neighborhood that we're spoken for. The human sex act has an emotional and psychological component so that we'll pair-bond and stay together to raise our very needy young for an extended period. I'm always fascinated by people's animal motivations.

CAST AND CREW CREDITS

PARAMOUNT PICTURES AND DREAMWORKS PICTURES Present
An AMBLIN ENTERTAINMENT/CRUISE|WAGNER Production
A STEVEN SPIELBERG Film

TOM CRUISE

WAR OF THE WORLDS

DAKOTA FANNING   MIRANDA OTTO   AND   TIM ROBBINS

Casting by
DEBRA ZANE
AND TERRI TAYLOR

Special Visual Effects and
Animation by
**INDUSTRIAL LIGHT &
MAGIC**

Senior Visual Effects Supervisor
DENNIS MUREN

Music by
JOHN WILLIAMS

Costume Designer
JOANNA JOHNSTON

Edited by
MICHAEL KAHN, A.C.E.

Production Designer
RICK CARTER

Director of Photography
JANUSZ KAMINSKI, ASC

Executive Producer
PAULA WAGNER

Produced by
**KATHLEEN KENNEDY
COLIN WILSON**

Based on the novel by
H.G. WELLS

Screenplay by
JOSH FRIEDMAN
AND DAVID KOEPP

Directed by
STEVEN SPIELBERG

CAST

Ray . . . . TOM CRUISE
Rachel . . . . DAKOTA FANNING
Mary Ann . . . . MIRANDA OTTO
Robbie . . . . JUSTIN CHATWIN
Harlan Ogilvy . . . . TIM ROBBINS
Vincent . . . . RICK GONZALEZ
Julio . . . . YUL VÁZQUEZ
Manny The Mechanic . . . LENNY VENITO
Bartender . . . . LISA ANN WALTER
Grandmother . . . . ANN ROBINSON
Grandfather . . . . GENE BARRY
Tim . . . . DAVID ALAN BASCHE
Herself . . . . ROZ ABRAMS
TV Reporter - Osaka . . . .
. . . . MICHAEL BROWNLEE
News Producer . . . . CAMILLIA SANES
News Cameraman . . . . MARLON YOUNG
News Van Driver . . . . . . JOHN EDDINS
Hatch Boss/Load Manager . . PETER GERETY
Dock Worker . . . . . . DAVID HARBOUR
Brazilian Neighbor . . . .
. . . . MIGUEL ANTONIO FERRER
Brazilian Neighbor's Wife . . JANUARY LAVOY

Neighbor with Lawnmower . . . .
. . . . STEPHEN GEVEDON
Woman . . . . JULIE WHITE
Hysterical Woman . . . MARIANNI EBERT
Mechanic's Assistant . . . RAFAEL SARDINA
Neighbor with Toddler . . . . . AMY RYAN
Intersection Guys . . . . ED VASSALLO
. . . . MICHAEL ARTHUR
Intersection Guy Cop . . . . DANNY HOCH
Man Studying Street . . . SHARRIEFF PUGH
Photographers . . . . ERIKA LAVONN
. . . . CHRISTOPHER EVAN WELCH
Men Holding Women . . . .
. . . . JOHN MICHAEL BOLGER
. . . . OMAR JERMAINE
Guy In Suit . . . . . . ROBERT CICCHINI
Bus Driver . . . . JIM HANNA
Crowd Onlookers . . . . . . TRACY HOWE,
. . . . . ADAM LAZARRE-WHITE, VITO
D'AMBROSIO, LAURA ZOE QUIST,
ANA MARIA QUINTANA, LORELEI LLEE
Ferry Worker . . . . MARK MANLEY
Ferry Captain . . . . JOHN SCURTI

Disaster Relief Volunteer. . . . .
BECKY ANN BAKER
Mother . . . . . . MARIANN MAYBERRY
3 Year Old Boy . . . . TY SIMPKINS
Smart Guy . . . . JERRY WALSH
National Guardsmen. . . TOMMY GUIFFRE
DANIEL FRANZESE
Older Man . . . . ED SCHIFF
Woman from Upstate. . . . . ELLEN BARRY
Panicky Woman. . . . . AMY HOHN
Informative Guy . . . . . . DANIEL ZISKIE
Ill-Informed Guy. . . . . . DAVID CONLEY
Conspiracy Buff. . . . DANIEL ERIC GOLD
Conspiracy Debunker . . . .
BOOKER T. WASHINGTON
Upset Mother. . . . . MAGGIE LACEY
Doomsday Guy . . . . ERIC ZUCKERMAN
Younger Man . . . . . DANIEL A. JACOBS
Woman in Crowd . . . ASHA R. NANAVATI
Young Soldier in Tank . . . .
JOAQUIN PEREZ-CAMPBELL
Well Meaning Mother . . DENDRIE TAYLOR
Well Meaning Father . . JAMES DUMONT
War of the Worlds Soldiers . . . .
TRAVIS AARON WADE, BENNY
CIARAMELLO, RICKY LUNA,
COLUMBUS SHORT, KENT FAULCON
Marine Majors . . . . KEVIN COLLINS
TERRY THOMAS
Airforce Pilot . . . . . CLAY BRINGHURST
Army Private. . . . . . JORGE-LUIS PALLO
Businesswomen. . . . . . . SUANNE SPOKE
KIRSTEN NELSON
Older Women. MELODY GARRETTLAURI
JOHNSON, TAKAYO FISCHER
Teenagers . . . . SHANNA COLLINS
ELIZABETH JAYNE HONG
Men in Baskets . . . . . ART CHUDABALA,
JEFFREY HUTCHINSON, DEMPSEY
PAPPION, CHRIS TODD
Boston Soldiers. . . JOHNNY KASTL, JUAN
CARLOS HERNANDEZ, BRUCE W.
DERDOSKI, JR., JOHN N. MORALES
Narration. . . . . . . MORGAN FREEMAN
Stunt Coordinator. . . . VIC ARMSTRONG
Assistant Stunt Coordinator . . . . JOEY BOX
Stuntman for Mr. Cruise . . CASEY O'NEILL
Stunts . . . . . GEORGE AGUILAR, WADE
ALLEN, BRUCE ARMSTRONG, NINA
ALMOND ARMSTRONG, SCOTT ARM-
STRONG, RICHARD BUCHER,
RICHARD BURDEN, JENNIFER
CAPUTO, DOUG CROSBY, KOFI ELAM,
PETER EPSTEIN, TANNER GILL,

AL GOTO, CORT HESSLER, TOBY
HOLGUIN, TERRY JACKSON, CRAIG
JENSEN, J.E. JOHNSON, THEO KYPRI,
HEIDI MONEYMAKER, JIM PALMER,
BUSTER REEVES, SIERRA RILEY
MORTAN, DENNIS SCOTT,
SHAWNNA THIBODEAU
Helicopter Pilot . . . . AL CERULLO

CREDITS

Visual Effects Supervisor. . PABLO HELMAN
Unit Production Manager . . . DAVID WITZ
Unit Production Manager . . . .
JONATHAN FILLEY
First Assistant Director . . . ADAM SOMNER
Second Assistant Director . . . . IAN STONE
Second Assistant Director. . . . .
JENNIFER TRUELOVE
ILM Animation Supervisor. . . . .
RANDY M. DUTRA
ILM Visual Effects Producer . . . .
SANDRA SCOTT
Supervising Sound Editor/Sound Designer . .
RICHARD KING
Re-Recording Mixers. . . . ANDY NELSON
ANNA BEHLMER
Production Supervisor . . . JASON MCGATLIN
Supervising Art Director . . . TONY FANNING
Art Directors . . . . DOUGLAS MEERDINK
ANDREW MENZIES
NORMAN NEWBERRY
Set Decorator . . . . ANNE KULJIAN
Camera Operators . . . . . . MITCH DUBIN
GEORGE BILLINGER
First Assistant Photographer . . . .
STEVEN MEIZLER
Second Assistant Photographer. . . . .
TOM JORDAN
"B" First Assistant Photographer. . . . .
MARK SPATH
"B" Second Assistant Photographer . . . . . .
DAVID O'BRIEN
Film Loader . . . . PAUL TOOMEY
Libra Mount Operator . . . . JON PHILION
Script Supervisor. . ANA MARIA QUINTANA
Sound Mixer . . . . . . RONALD JUDKINS
Boom Operator. . . . . ROBERT JACKSON
Cable Person. . . . . PEGGY NAMES
Video Assist . . . . . . DANIEL P. MOORE
Chief Lighting Technician . . DAVID DEVLIN
Assistant Chief Lighting Technician . . . . . .
LARRY RICHARDSON
Chief Rigging Electrician . . BRIAN LUKAS

Assistant Chief Rigging Electrician . . . . . .
MARK MELE
Electricians . . . . DAN MCMAHON,
MAREK BOJSZA, ROBERT ALLEN, JR.,
DAMON LIEBOWITZ, SEAN GINN,
JUAN C. TRUJILLO
First Company Grip . . JIM KWIATKOWSKI
Second Company Grip . . . .
STEVE O'HOLLEARN
First Company Rigging Grip . . . .
CHARLEY H. GILLERAN
Second Company Rigging Grip . . . .
KEVIN FAHEY
Dolly Grip Operator . . . . JOHNNY MANG
"B" Dolly Grip Operator . . RALPH SCHERER
Grips . . JAMIE FRANTA, BODIE HYMAN,
ALEX KLABUKOV, WILLIAM BOONE III
Technocrane Operator . . CARLOS GONZALEZ
Property Master . . . DOUG HARLOCKER
Assistant Property Master . . . .
SCOTT GETZINGER
Special Effects Coordinator . . DANIEL SUDICK
Special Effects Supervisors . . DAVID BLITSTEIN
GINTAR REPECKA
Special Effects Forepersons . . . .
ROBERT L. OLMSTEAD, TODD JENSEN
Special Effects Buyer . . . SARA R. MORRIS
Special Effects Technicians . . STEVE AUSTIN,
DAVID ELAND, ERIC COOK,
RON MATHEWS, KEVIN BOWERS,
KEITH HAYNES, ROY AUGENSTEIN,
LENNY DALRYMPLE,
RODERIC "MICKEY" DUFF
Special Effects Model Maker Foreperson . . . .
DAMACIO CORTEZ, JR.
Location Manager . . . .
COLLEEN HILARY GIBBONS
Assistant Location Manager . . . .
LEANN E. EMMERT
Lead Persons . . . . . JONATHAN BOBBITT
JENNIFER LAGURA
On-Set Dresser . . . . ERIC J. LULING
Set Dressers . . . BART BARBUSCIA, LOUIS
TERRY, GIOVANNI BIANCHINI,
SHANNON BROCK, CHRISTOPHER L.
FUENTES, AL LEWIS
Assistant Costume Designer . . . .
ROBERT WOJEWODSKI
Costume Supervisor . . . . PAMELA J. WISE
Key Costumers . . . . . DIANA J. WILSON
LINDA REDMON
Costumers . . . . PETER WHITE,
LISA BOJARSKI, N. EDWARD FINCHER

Set Costumers . . . . EVA L. PRAPPAS,
COOKIE LOPEZ, GREGORY B. PEÑA,
ALISON GAIL BIXBY, BRAD HOLTZMAN,
DANIELLE WAIT
Key Tailor . . . . CONCEPCION GAXIOLA
Costumer to Mr. Cruise . . KENDALL ERRAIR
Dyer . . . . CAROL DEMARTI
Ager . . . . DOMINICK DERASMO
Makeup Department Head . . . LOIS BURWELL
Key Makeup . . . . . KENNETH R. MYERS
Makeup Artists . . LEO COREY CASTELLANO
TINA HARRELSON
Prosthetics Fabrication . . . . JOEL HARLOW
ROB HINDERSTEIN
Hair Department Head . . . .
KATHRYN BLONDELL
Key Hairstylist . . . AUDREY L. ANZURES
Hairstylist to Mr. Cruise . . . .
KATHARINE KREMP
First Assistant Editor . . . PATRICK CRANE
Assistant Editors . . SAM SEIG, MIKE CUEVAS,
MIKE WILSON, MARK GILLARD,
CRAIG HAYES
Apprentice Editor . . . . . SILJA TONISSON
Post Production Assistant . . . .
MICHAEL PEDRAZA
New York Casting Associate . . . .
LOIS J. DRABKIN
Los Angeles Casting Associate . . . .
TANNIS VALLELY
Casting Assistant . . . . JOCELYN THOMAS
Background Casting . . . . . SANDE ALESSI
Assistant Art Directors . . . . CURT BEECH,
EASTON SMITH, LORI ROWBOTHAM
GRANT, PAUL SONSKI,
TODD CHERNIAWSKY
Concept Illustrators . . . . . . JAMES CLYNE
CHRISTOPHER BAKER
Storyboard Artist . . . . . . DAVID LOWERY
Previsualization Supervisor . . DAN GREGOIRE
Previsualization . . DORIAN BUSTAMANTE,
EUISUNG LEE, E. BRAD ALEXANDER,
NICK MARKEL
Art Department Coordinator . . . .
CEDAR MCCLURE
Assistant Art Department Coordinator . . . . .
MARK TAYLOR
Senior Researcher . . . . . JESSICA BIGGINS
Researcher . . . STEPHEN CHRISTENSEN
Military Technical Advisor . . . MAJ. JOSEPH
TODD BREASSEALE
Associate to Mr. Spielberg . . . .
KRISTIE MACOSKO

Assistants to Mr. Spielberg . . BEN BOHLING
ELIZABETH NYE
Production Assistant to Mr. Spielberg . . . . .
RYAN SUFFERN
Executive Assistant to Ms. Wagner . . . .
GRADY LEE
Assistant to Ms. Wagner . . . ARIK RUCHIM
Associate to Ms. Kennedy . . . ELYSE KLAITS
Production Assistant to Ms. Kennedy . . . . .
CHRISTOPHER BUDDY
Associate to Mr. Wilson. . JENNIFER TEVES
Assistant to Mr. Wilson. . . . .
BENJAMIN SHIFFRIN
Executive Assistant to Mr. Cruise. . . SUE FREY
Production Coordinator. . CANDICE CAMPOS
Assistant Production Coordinators . . . .
MARK SWENSON, LORI BERLANGA,
JENNIFER WEBB
Production Secretary. . . . JASON ZORIGIAN
Second Second Assistant Director . . . .
TIMOTHY R. PRICE
DGA Trainee . . . . JENNY NOLAN
Production Assistants . . . . SARAH E. BAKER,
IAN CALIP, KYLE COOKMEYER,
LAUREN DANDRIDGE, KATHRYN
GALBERTH, GABE GERBER, JARED
GOODE, MATTHEW GORDON,
MATTHEW LOMBARDO, MICHAEL
MILLER, STEVEN OPPENHEIM, JESSICA
RIPKA, BRETT ROBINSON, CLINT SCOTT,
FRANCESCO TIGNINI, KEVIN WALSH
Unit Publicist . . . . DEBORAH WULIGER
Still Photographer . . . ANDREW COOPER
Medic . . . . AHMED SAKER
Production Auditor . . . . TIM L. PEARSON
First Assistant Auditors . . . .
MICHAEL B. BEAUDIN
ALEXA SONG LINDENTHALER
Assistant Auditors . . . WILLIAM J. OAKS III,
JAMES D'DAMERY, JR., JANINE SCHIRO,
CARLO PRATTO
Payroll Auditor . . . . GABRIELA ORTEGA
Construction Estimator . . . .
LAURIE ARNOW-EPSTEIN
Construction Auditor . . EMILY TAKEHARA
Auditing Assistant . . . . DAVID IACCH
Marine Coordinator . . . .
CAPTAIN TROY WATERS
Assistant Marine Coordinator . . . .
MATTHEW O'CONNOR
Post Production Executive . . MARTIN COHEN
Post Production Supervisor . . STEPHANIE ITO
Associate Post Production Coordinator. . . . .
ROB YAMAMOTO

Post Production Coordinator. . . . .
SAMANTHA BECKER
First Assistant Sound Editors . . . .
LINDA YEANEY, ANDREW BOCK
Additional Sound Design and Editing . . . . .
MICHAEL BABCOCK, AARON
GLASCOCK, HAMILTON STERLING
Sound Effects Editors . . . .
MICHAEL W. MITCHELL, PIERO MURA
Sound Effects Recordists . . . .
JOHN PAUL FASAL, ERIC POTTER
Dialogue Editors . . . . HUGO WENG
MICHAEL MAGILL
ADR Supervisor . . . . R.J. KIZER
ADR Editors . . . . LAURA GRAHAM
LINDA FOLK
ADR Mixer . . . . . CHARLEEN STEEVES
ADR Recordist . . . . . DAVID LUCARELLI
ADR Stage Engineer . . . . DEREK CASARI
Foley Supervisor . . CHRISTOPHER FLICK
Foley Editors . . . . MARK PAPPAS
JONATHAN KLEIN
Foley Mixer . . . . BRIAN RUBERG
Supervising Foley Artist . . . GARY HECKER
Foley Artist. . . . MICHAEL BROOMBERG
Voice Casting . . . . . CAITLIN MCKENNA
Assistant Sound Editors . . . .
MONIQUE SALVATO
CHARLIE CAMPAGNA
RAY MALDONADO
Additional Sound Mixing . . ELLIOT TYSON
D.M. HEMPHILL
Recordists . . . . ROBERT RENGA, CRAIG
"PUP" HEATH, MATT PATTERSON
Re-Recording Engineers . . . .
DENIS ST. AMAND, PAUL PAVELKA
Post Production Facilities Provided by . . . . .
20TH CENTURY FOX STUDIOS
Additional Sound Design Services by
SKYWALKER SOUND
A LUCASFILM LTD. COMPANY
MARIN COUNTY, CALIFORNIA
Additional Sound Design . . RANDY THOM
Sound Editor . . . . . . RICHARD HYMNS
Sound Effects Editor . . ADDISON TEAGUE
Assistant Sound Designer . WILLIAM E. FILES
Amblin Projectionist . . . RENE GONZALEZ
Orchestrations. . . . . . . CONRAD POPE
EDDIE KARAM
Music Editor . . . . PETER MYLES
Music Scoring Mixer . . SHAWN MURPHY
Music Contractor . . SANDY DE CRESCENT
Chorus . . HOLLYWOOD FILM CHORALE
Vocal Coordinator . . . . . SALLY STEVENS

Music Preparation . . . .
    JO ANN KANE MUSIC SERVICE
Scoring Crew . . . . SUSAN MCLEAN,
ADAM MICHALAK, MARK ESHELMAN,
GREG LOSKORN, BRYAN CLEMENTS,
    ROBERT WOLFF
Music Recorded and Mixed at . . . . . SONY
PICTURES STUDIOS, CULVER CITY, CA
Set Designers . . . . . KEVIN CROSS, BILLY
HUNTER, ARIC CHENG, SCOTT
HERBERTSON, ROY BARNES
Model Makers . . . . . . JEFF FROST, RON
MENDELL, GREGORY JEIN
Construction Coordinator . . . .
    JOHN V. VILLARINO
Construction Foreperson . . . BOBBY MARA
Paint Forepersons . . . . RICHARD GIROD,
WILLIAM GIROD, SHARON BARNEBY
Sculptor Foreperson . . . FRED ARBEGAST
Head Labor Foreperson. EDDIE CALDERON
Plaster Forepersons . . . . TODD BENNETT
    LOUIS MARQUIS
Carpenter Forepersons . . . . KENT SVERRE
DYSTHE, BRIAN FEOLA, JAMES
PERSON, JOHN SORIA, ROB
"HERMAN" WILLIAMSON, PETE
YOUDS, JIM PIKE, ROGER SMITHSON
Labor Forepersons . . ANTHONY J. FEOLA,
TY BECK, MICHAEL DUPUIS, DAN
SIMON, EDMUND ACUNA, JOSEPH
ESPOSITO, PETE "PEANUT" MEDINA
On-Set Painter. . . . CHRIS ZIMMERMAN
Sculptor Sub-Foreperson . . . CRAIG ABELE
Greens Supervisor. . . . RANDY MARTENS
Chief Greens Forepersons APRIL MARTENS,
    JASON VANOVER
Greens Foreperson . . . . CHRIS SCHMID
On-Set Greens Foreperson . STEVE SICKELS
Greens Sub-Forepersons . . . . . . TERENCE
CORLISS, DAVID PAUL CORRAL
Transportation Coordinator . . . .
    TOMMY TANCHAROEN
Transportation Captains . . . . MAXWELL R.
JOHNSON II, THOMAS WHELPLEY
Transportation Dispatcher . . . .
    AUDREY A. CONRAD
Catering By . . . . FOR STARS CATERING
Craft Service . . . . NICK MESTRANDREA
Production Security Provided By . . SISS LTD

NEW YORK UNIT
Production Supervisor . . . .
    GREGORY H. ALPERT

Art Directors . . . . TOM WARREN
    EDWARD PISONI
Assistant Set Decorators. . PAUL CHEPONIS,
    REGINA GRAVES, S.D.S.A.
"B" Camera Operator . . MICHAEL GREEN
"B" Second Assistant Photographer . . . . . .
    JAMIESON K. FITZPATRICK
Film Loader . . . . CHRISTIAN HOLLYER
Script Supervisor. . . . . LUCA KOUIMELIS
Boom Operator . . . . . DAN ROSENBLUM
Cable Person. . . . . RICHARD A. MADER
Chief Lighting Technician . . JIM RICHARDS
Assistant Chief Lighting Technician . . . . . .
    WILLIAM ALMEIDA
Chief Rigging Electrician . . . .
    CLAY LIVERSIDGE
First Company Grip . . . .
    CHARLIE MARROQUIN
Second Company Grip. . . PAUL CANDRILLI
Dolly Grip Operator . . . .
    LUIS "RICK" MARROQUIN
Property Master . . . . . . PETER GELFMAN
Assistant Property Master . . JAMES V. KENT
Prop Shop Foreperson . . . DAVID GAGNON
Special Effects Supervisor . . CONNIE BRINK
Location Manager . . . . . LYN PINEZICH
Assistant Location Manager. . . . .
    MICHAEL KRIARIS
Lead Person . . . . DAVID WEINMAN
Set Dressing Foreperson . . . CHRIS VOGT
On-Set Dressers . . . . . JOANN ATWOOD
    JOSEPH M. DELUCA
Costume Supervisors. . DONNA MALONEY
    AMY ROTH
Set Costumers. . . . . . PAMELA AARON,
BENJAMIN WILSON, MICKEY
CARLETON, CARMIA MARSHALL
Key Makeup. . . . . LINDA GRIMES
Key Hairstylist . . . . . JERRY DECARLO
Background Casting . . . . . BILLY DOWD
Assistant Art Directors . . . DAVID SWAYZE,
DAN KUCHAR, MICHAEL AUSZURA,
MIGUEL LOPEZ-CASTILLO,
CHARLES E. MCCARRY, MARION
KOLSBY, DOUGLAS HUSZTI
Graphic Designers . . . . MARK BACHMAN
    JOAN WINTERS
Art Department Coordinator. . . . .
    GLENN LLOYD
Production Coordinator. . GREG OUTCALT
Assistant Production Coordinator . . . .
    PHILIP A. RAMOS
Production Secretaries. . . . MONICA CELIS
BARRAZA, SUSAN ORGA

Second Second Assistant Director . . . . . .
　　　　　　　　　ERIC LASKO
DGA Trainee . . . . DANIEL FERNANDEZ
Production Assistants . . . JAMIE BUCKNER,
　　NICHOLAS CARR, MICHAEL EBERLY,
　　NATHAN GRUBB, AARON KOESON,
　　JOHN KOUROMIHELAKIS, MATTHEW
　　MASON, AARON Z. SCHOR, LUKE J.
　　SMITH, JENNIFER SOKOLOV, EVE
　　STRICKMAN, AJAMU WALKER,
　　　　　　BRADLEY WEINRIEB
Still Photographer . . FRANK MASI, S.M.P.S.P
Medic . . . . KATHY COSSU
Craft Service . . . .
　McKENNA BROTHERS CRAFT SERVICE
Assistant Auditors . . . . . REBECCA GLEW,
　　KELLY O'BIER, JAMES HINTON,
　　　　　　　RICHARD MAST
Payroll Auditor . . LAURA KREFT CARABALLO
Construction Auditor . . JEREMY D. PRATT
Auditing Assistant . . . . . . RYAN VINIOTIS
Construction Coordinator . . . RAY SAMITZ
Construction Forepersons . . GERARD J. FUREY
　　　　　RICHARD BRYAN DOUGLAS
Chief Electrician . . . ROBERTO JIMENEZ
Electric Foreperson . . . MIGUEL JIMENEZ
Electricians . . . . PAUL STEINBERG
　　　　　　　　CHRIS ZIZZO
Construction Shop Manager . . . .
　　　　　　　JEREMIAH SELLITTI
On-Set Painter . . . . . M. TONY TROTTA
Scenic Artist . . . . ROBERT TOPOL
Chief Greensperson . . . LARRY AMANUEL
Transportation Captain . . STEVE HAMMOND
Transportation Co-Captains . . PETER CLORES
　　　　　　　WILLIAM J. MCFADDEN
Transportation Coordinators . GENE O'NEILL
　　　　　　　　LORI PERNAL

VIRGINIA UNIT
Art Director . . . . DAVID CRANK
Lead Person . . . . . . KENNETH BRYANT
Set Dresser . . . . TAYLOR REESE
Assistant Chief Rigging Electrician . . . . . .
　　　　　　　　DONALD AROS
Rigging Electricians . DAVID SHANE GUILD
　　　　　　　RUSSELL A. WICKS
Rigging Grips . . . . . . PAUL BOGDAN III
　　　　　　　　JOSH CROSS
Chief Special Effects Technician . . . .
　　　　　　　GARY PILKINGTON
Special Effects Technicians . . . . . WILLIAM
　　CATANIA, THOMAS FIFE, TOM
　　TURNBULL, JEFF ZOOK

Assistant Location Manager . . . .
　　　　　　　LAURA BERNING
Costume Supervisor . . . . . . DEB DALTON
Background Casting . . JEANNE BOISINEAU
Production Coordinator . . ELLEN GANNON
Production Secretaries . . RACHEL HURLEY,
　　　　　CHRISTOPHER D. MENKE
Production Assistants . . . MEGAN HELSLEY
　　　　　　　　LUCAS KROST
Additional Second Assistant Director . . . . .
　　　　　　　　JANE FERGUSON
Assistant Auditor . CATHERINE M. ALLEBE
Construction Coordinator . . . .
　　　　　　RICHARD BLANKENSHIP
Construction Forepersons . . . .
　JIMMY L. CARMICKLE, JOE HARPER
Lead Painter . . . . . RICHARD SALINAS
Chief Greensperson . . . MARK D. KERSEY
Greens Foreperson . . . CRAIG M. TAYLOR
Transportation Captain . . . TOM MAWYER
Transportation Coordinator . . . .
　　　　　　　JENNIFER WEILAND
Visual Effects Producer . . . CARI THOMAS
Visual Effects Coordinator . . . .
　　　　　　　CONNIE KENNEDY
Visual Effects Plate Coordinator . . . .
　　　　　　　　STEVE RIERA
Special Visual Effects and Animation By
INDUSTRIAL LIGHT & MAGIC
a Lucasfilm Ltd. Company
Marin County, California
Digital Production Supervisor . . . .
　　　　　　　CURT MIYASHIRO
TD Supervisor . . . . MICHAEL DI COMO
Compositing Supervisor . . . .
　　　　　　　MARSHALL KRASSER
Associate Animation Supervisors . . . . JENN
　　EMBERLY, TIM HARRINGTON
Sequence Supervisors . . . ROBERT MARINIC,
　　PAT BRENNAN, JAY COOPER, RAUL
　　ESSIG, ERIK KRUMREY, NIGEL
　　SUMNER, JEFF SUTHERLAND
Visual Effects Art Director . . . .
　　　　　　CHRISTIAN ALZMANN
Creature Development Supervisor . . . .
　　　　　　　TIM MCLAUGHLIN
Digital Model Supervisors . . . .
　MICHAEL KOPERWAS, RUSSELL PAUL
Visual Effects Editor . . . . MIKE GLEASON
Lead Inferno Artist . . . . . CHAD TAYLOR
Lead Digital Matte Artist . . . JOSHUA ONG
Lead CG Layout Artist . . TERRY CHOSTNER
Lead Digital Paint & Roto Artist . . . .
　　　　　　　AMY SHEPARD

Additional Visual Effects Supervisors . . . . . . ED HIRSH, KIM LIBRERI
Visual Effects Directors of Photography . . . . MARTY ROSENBERG, KIM MARKS
Model/Miniature Supervisor . . . . STEVE GAWLEY
Visual Effects Associate Producer . . . . LORI ARNOLD
Senior Animators . . C. MICHAEL EASTON DAVE SIDLEY
Animators . . . . . . IZZY ACAR, GEORGE ALECO-SIMA, CHARLES ALLENECK, DERRICK CARLIN, MARC CHU, PETER KELLY, SHAWN KELLY, GLEN McINTOSH, PHIL MCNALLY, RICK O'CONNOR, DAVID SHIRK, DELIO TRAMONTOZZI, CHI CHUNG TSE, ANDY WONG
TD's . . . . TIM BELSHER, JEFFREY BENEDICT, ARON BONAR, MATTHEW BOUCHARD, AMANDA BRAGGS, STEVE BRAGGS, TRIPP BROWN, LYDIA CHOY, ZACHARY COLE, PAUL CHURCHILL, RICHARD DUCKER, LEANDRO ESTEBECORENA, THOMAS FEJES, HOWARD GERSH, JEFF GREBE, INDIRA GUERRIERI, GERALD GUTSCHMIDT, CHRISTOPHE HERY, NEIL HERZINGER, PEG HUNTER, RUSSELL KOONCE, GREGOR LAKNER, LANA LAN, JEROEN LAPRE, JOSHUA LEVINE, PHILIP METSCHAN, MARIE-LAURE NGUYEN, MASAYORI OKA, JAMIE PILGRIM, RICARDO RAMOS, MICHAEL RICH, JASON ROSSON, JAMES ROWELL, ANTHONY SHAFER, JOHN SIGURDSON, DANIEL SLAVIN, DAMIAN STEEL, BLAKE SWEENEY, ERIC TEXIER, VINCENT TOSCANO
Digital Compositors . . MIMI ABERS, LEAH ANTON, OKAN ATAMAN, JOEL BEHRENS, CATHY BURROW, KELA CABRALES, COLIN CAMPBELL, BRIAN CONNOR, DON CRAWFORD, JEFF DORAN, BILL EYLER, CONNY FAUSER, JASON HILL, SHERRY HITCH, ROBERT HOFFMEISTER, HEATHER HOYLAND, MICHAEL JAMIESON, STEPHEN KENNEDY, WILL McCOY, JENNIFER McKNEW, TOM ROSSETER, BARRY SAFLEY, JEFF SUTHERLAND, RUSS SUEYOSHI, TODD VAZIRI, THOMAS ZILS
Inferno Artists . . . MARK CASEY, CAITLIN CONTENT, SAM EDWARDS, ADAM HOWARD, KEVIN MAY, SEBASTIEN MOREAU, BEN O'BRIEN, ALEX TROPIEC, RITA ZIMMERMAN
Digital Matte Artists . . VANESSA CHEUNG, YANICK DUSSEAULT, BRIAN FLORA, PAUL HUSTON, BRYANT GRIFFIN, BENJAMIN HUBER, MASAHIKO TANI, WEI ZHENG
Digital Models . . . . JEAN BOLTE, JON BONNENFANT, JON FARMER, BRIDGET GOODMAN, FRANK GRAVATT, JUNG-SEUNG HONG, GIOVANNI NAKPIL, MARK SIEGEL, TONY SOMMERS, DONNA TENNIS, HOWIE WEED, SUNNY WEI, ELBERT YEN
Creature Development Artists . . . . DUGAN BEACH, MARTIN COVEN, MICHELLE DEAN, COREY ROSEN, RENITA TAYLOR, TIM WADDY, GREG WEINER, KEIJI YAMAGUCHI, JOHN ZDANKIEWICZ
ILM Creature Design . . . RYAN CHURCH, CARLOS HUANTE, SANGJUN LEE
Lead Location Data Capture . . . . DUNCAN BLACKMAN
Location Data Capture . . JOHN WHISNANT
Layout Technical Lead . . JEFF SALTZMANN
CG Layout Artists . . . . . COLIN BENOIT MELISSA MULLIN
Matchmove Artists . . . . LANNY CERMAK, SELWYN EDDY III, WOONAM KIM, KERRY LEE, LUKE LONGIN, DAVID MANOS MORRIS, JOE STEVENSON, ROLAND YEPEZ, MARIA GOODALE
Digital Paint & Roto Artists . . . . ERIC CHRISTENSEN, NIKA DUNNE, MICHAELA CALANCHINI CARTER, DAWN GATES, DREW KLAUSNER, LAUREN MORIMOTO, KATIE MORRIS, MICHELLE MOTTA, MICHAEL VAN EPS, ERIN WEST, HEIDI ZABIT
Production Manager . . . . MONIQUE GOUGEON-DI COMO
Visual Effects Coordinators . DALE TAYLOR, GORDON WITTMANN, KRIS WRIGHT
Visual Effects Production Assistants . . . . . . BLAKE NICKLE, SEAN RODRIGUEZ, DELIA STONE
Assistant Editor . . . . JAMES MILTON
VFX First Assistant Camera Operators . . . . . ROBERT HILL, VANCE PIPER
Senior Model Makers . . CHARLIE BAILEY, DON BIES, BRIAN DEWE, ROBBIE M. EDWARDS, LORNE PETERSON

Model/Miniature Makers. . . . . NICHOLAS BOGLE, PHIL BROTHERTON, MARK BUCK, JOHN DUNCAN, TODD FELLOWS, JON FOREMAN, NELSON HALL, NEAL HALTER, PIERRE MAURER, SCOTT MCNAMARA, MITCH ROMANAUSKI, MICHAEL STEFFE, TOM VUKMANIC, DANNY WAGNER

Lead Model/Miniature Painter. . . . . PEGGY HRASTAR

Model/Miniature Painters . . . . LAUREN ABRAMS, VICTORIA LEWIS, RANDY OTTENBERG, MELANIE WALAS

Practical Effects Supervisors . . . . ROBBIE CLOT, GEOFF HERON

Practical Effects Technicians . ROGER DODD, PHILIP HERON, WILLIAM MOORE, THOMAS RENIA, RICHARD SPAH, FRANK TARANTINO

Stage Technicians . . . . . WILLIAM BARR, DAVID CHILDERS, THOMAS CLOUTIER, RICHARD DEMOLSKI, HARRY O'HARE, CRAIG MOHAGEN, MICHAEL OLAGUE, FRANK STRZALKOWSKI

Model Shop Coordinator . KEVIN WALLACE

Video Assist . ANDREW NEDDERMEYER

Research and Development . . . . PHILIP HUBBARD, JASON JOHNSON, ERIC SCHAFER

Production & Technical Support . . . . LORI CASLER, JAYESH DALAL, BRIAN FONG, CYRUS JAM, JIM RANDELL, RYAN SMITH, THADDEUS PARKINSON, ROBIN YOUNG

Production Accountant . . . SUSAN MACKE

ILM Senior Staff . . . LYNWEN BRENNAN CHRISSIE ENGLAND

Visual Effects Executive Producer . . . . JUDITH WEAVER

Concept Design By. . . . . DOUG CHIANG AND ICE BLINK STUDIOS

Concept Artists . . . . . MARC GABBANA, RANDY GAUL, KURT KAUFMAN

CG Artists . . . . PETE BILLINGTON YOUNG DUK CHO

Hero Weed and Live Action Crashed Tripod Effects By STAN WINSTON STUDIO

Effects Supervisors. . LINDSAY MACGOWAN ALAN SCOTT

Special Effects Coordinator . . SHANE MAHAN

Scenic Key Artists . . . AARON SIMS, JOHN CHEREVKA, HIROSHI KATAGIRI, GREG MCDOUGALL, MARK MAITRE,

DAVID MERRITT, TONY MEININGER, EDWARD LAWTON, KEN CORONET, TREVOR HENSLEY, TED HAINES, JAMIE GROVE

Key Technicians . . KEITH MARBORY, IAN STEPHENSON, CARI FINKEN, CLARK JAMES, CHRISTIAN RISTOW

Fake Bodies By . . . . . STEVE JOHNSON

Color Timer . . . . DALE GRAHN

Negative Cutter . . . . . . GARY BURRITT

Dolby Sound Consultant. . . . JIM WRIGHT

Main and End Title Design . PICTURE MILL

Opticals By . . . . PACIFIC TITLE

Soundtrack Available On DECCA

"FLATLINE"
By Jeffrey Scott Harber, Jayce Alexander Basques, William Peng & Drew Dehaven Hall
Performed By Aphasia
Courtesy Of Luke Eddins at Luke Hits
And Joint Venture Recordings

"NOBODY MOVE"
By Benjamin Mallon, Michael Ashby, William Sherwin, Eric Joy, Omari Edwards & Glenn Kuchenbeiser
Performed By Capstone
Courtesy Of Luke Eddins at Luke Hits

"SAILOR MOON BGM"
By Arisawa Takanori
Courtesy Of DIC Music, LLC
And Columbia Music Entertainment, Inc.

"ENIGMA VIBE 2"
Written & Performed By Nicholas Carr
Courtesy Of Nickelodeon

"FA WAT"
By Christopher Shawn King
Performed By Kriz Kang
Courtesy Of Luke Eddins at Luke Hits

"INFIERNO"
Written & Performed By Santino
Courtesy Of Luke Eddins at Luke Hits
And Anouk Zisa-Bongiovi

"IF I RULED THE WORLD"
By Leslie Bricusse & Cyril Ornadel
Performed By Tony Bennett
Courtesy Of Columbia Records
By Arrangement With SONY BMG Music Entertainment

"LITTLE DEUCE COUPE"
By Brian Wilson & Roger Christian

"HUSHABYE MOUNTAIN"
By Richard M. Sherman & Robert B. Sherman

"SpongeBob SquarePants" Provided By
NICKELODEON

"Sailor Moon" Courtesy Of
TOEI ANIMATION CO., LTD

We Gratefully Acknowledge The Cooperation
Of The Department Of Defense And
Specifically:

Mr. Philip Strub, Department Of Defense

The 10th Mountain Division (Light Infantry)
and Fort Drum, NY, US Army

The Virginia Army National Guard

The National Training Center and Fort Irwin,
CA, US Army

Maj. Jeffrey J. Nyhart, U.S. Marine Corps
Motion Picture & Television Office

1st Tank Battalion, 1st Marine Division,
Marine Corps Air
Ground Combat Center -
Twentynine Palms, CA

1st Light Armored Reconnaissance Battalion,
1st Marine Division, Camp Pendleton, CA

1st Lt. Mary B. Danner, U.S. Air Force
Entertainment Liaison Office

56th Fighter Wing, Luke Air Force Base, AZ

355th Wing, Davis-Monthan Air Force Base, AZ

U.S. Air Force Thunderbird Demonstration
Team, Nellis Air Force Base, NV

The Producers Wish To Thank The Following:
HITACHI, LTD.
AMERICAN RED CROSS

KODAK Motion Picture Film

Prints By TECHNICOLOR®

Color By DELUXE®

Filmed with PANAVISION® Cameras
and Lenses

WarOfTheWorlds.com

ABOUT THE SCREENWRITERS

JOSH FRIEDMAN (written by) is also the author of the screenplay *The Black Dahlia*, based on the novel by James Ellroy, currently in production with director Brian De Palma. His screenplay *Orphan's Dawn* is in development at 20th Century Fox. A graduate of Brown University, he lives in Los Angeles with his wife and child.

DAVID KOEPP (written by) has written and directed the films *Secret Window, Stir of Echoes, The Trigger Effect,* and *Suspicious.* He wrote or co-wrote the films *Zathura, Spider-Man, Panic Room, Snake Eyes, The Lost World: Jurassic Park, Mission: Impossible, The Paper, Jurassic Park, Carlito's Way, Death Becomes Her, Bad Influence,* and *Apartment Zero.* Koepp was born in Wisconsin and went to film school at UCLA. He lives in New York City.